KT-368-605

THE SCANDINAVIAN ELEMENT
IN FRENCH AND NORMAN

G59/1076

THE
SCANDINAVIAN ELEMENT
IN FRENCH AND NORMAN

A Study of the Influence of the Scandinavian
Languages on French from the Tenth Century
to the Present

Ralph Paul de Gorog, Ph.D.

*Assistant Professor of Romance Languages and German
in the University of Georgia*

BOOKMAN ASSOCIATES

New York

EDINBURGH UNIVERSITY LIBRARY

CANCELLED

© 1958, by Ralph de Gorog

MANUFACTURED IN THE UNITED STATES OF AMERICA BY
UNITED PRINTING SERVICES, INC.
NEW HAVEN, CONN.

PREFACE

This book is based on the author's doctoral dissertation, "The Scandinavian Element in French and Norman." Since the time when the dissertation was accepted by the Faculty of Philosophy of Columbia University in 1954, the author has rewritten the entire work, eliminating historical material which can readily be found elsewhere, and reconsidering some of the etymologies presented. The author's original plan was to do for the Norse element in French what Marius Valkhoff did for the Dutch element in *Les Mots français d'origine néerlandaise*. After examining earlier studies of Norse influence in French and after considering the etymologies presented in most French dictionaries it became evident that lexicographers tended to repeat etymologies found in earlier works, often without questioning them. A study of the dictionaries of the Scandinavian languages reveals important information for the student of French etymology. Professor André Martinet, whose help and guidance made the present work possible, suggested that the author study the problem by reconsidering the etymologies in the light of phonetic chronology. Since the Norse words entered the Romance dialect of Neustria during the first decades of the 10th century, a study of the phonology of the French of that period, and the Scandinavian dialect introduced there, would certainly show whether a given word could have been introduced there at the time, and whether the word could have reached a certain stage in phonetic development if it had no history in France earlier than the 10th century. Therefore we shall examine the phonology of Old French and of Old Danish of that period and then discuss the treatment of each of the Scandinavian phonemes.

The author would like to express his gratitude to Professor André Martinet of the University of Paris for his interest in the present work and for his invaluable guidance, to M. Jean Adigard des Gautries of the Centre National de la Recherche Scientifique for his many kind suggestions, and to Professor Elliott Dobbie of Columbia University whose valuable criticism helped the author avoid many serious mistakes. Any errors which now remain are entirely those of the author.

CONTENTS

ABBREVIATIONS OF WORKS CITED

Alessio: Giovanni Alessio, *Grammatica Storica Francese*, I. Introduzione—Fonetica. Bari, 1951.

ALF: *Atlas linguistique de la France*, p. p. J. Gilliéron et E. Edmont, Paris, 1903-1910.

ALF, Supplément: *Atlas linguistique de la France, Supplément*, p. p. J. Gilliéron, Paris, 1921.

Barbier, *Miscellanea Lexicographica*: Paul Barbier, *Miscellanea Lexicographica*, Etymological and Lexical Notes on the French Language and on the Romance Dialects of France, in *Proceedings of the Leeds Philosophical Society*, Leeds, 1927-1952.

Battisti-Alessio: Carlo Battisti and Giovanni Alessio, *Dizionario etimologico italiano*, Florence, 1950-1952.

Björkman: Erik Björkman, *Scandinavian Loan-Words in Middle English*, Upsala, 1900.

Bloch: Oscar Bloch and W. von Wartburg, *Dictionnaire étymologique de la langue française*, 2nd edition, Paris, 1950.

Cleasby-Vigfusson: Richard Cleasby and Gudbrand Vigfusson, *An Icelandic-English Dictionary*, Oxford, 1874.

Cotgrave: Randle Cotgrave, *A Dictionarie of the French and English Tongues*, London, 1611 (reproduced by the University of South Carolina Press, Columbia, S. C., 1950).

Dauzat: A. Dauzat, *Dictionnaire étymologique de la langue française*, Paris, 1938.

David Ferrand: *La Muse Normande* de David Ferrand, ed. A. Héron, Rouen, 1894. Volume V contains a glossary.

Decorde: Abbé J.-E. Decorde, *Dictionnaire du patois du pays de Bray*, Paris-Rouen-Neufchatel, 1852.

DG: Adolphe Hatzfeld, Arsène Darmesteter and Antoine Thomas, *Dictionnaire général de la langue française*, 9th edition, Paris, 1932.

Du Bois: Louis Du Bois and J. Travers, *Glossaire du patois normand*, Caen, 1856.

Duméril: Édélestand and Alfred Duméril, *Dictionnaire du patois normand*, Caen, 1849.

Falk: H. Falk, "Altnordisches Seewesen," *Wörter und Sachen*, IV (1912), 1-122.

Falk-Torp: H. Falk and A. Torp, *Norwegisch-Dänisches Etymologisches Wörterbuch*, Heidelberg, 1910.

FEW: Walther von Wartburg, *Französisches Etymologisches Wörterbuch*, Bonn, Tübingen, 1928- .

Frahm: W. Frahm, *Das Meer und die Seefahrt in der altfranzösischen Literatur*, Göttingen, 1914.

Gamillscheg: E. Gamillscheg, *Etymologisches Wörterbuch der französischen Sprache*, Heidelberg, 1926-1928.

J. A. des Gautries: Gautries, Jean Adigard des, *Les Noms de personnes scandinaves en Normandie de 911 à 1066*, Nomina Germanica 11, Lund, 1954.

Godefroy: F. Godefroy, *Dictionnaire de l'ancienne langue française et de tous ses dialectes du IXe au XVe siècle*, Paris, 1886-1902. *Lexique de l'ancien français*, New York, 1928.

Gredig: Silvia Gredig, *Essai sur la formation du vocabulaire du skieur français*, Zurich, 1939.

Guerlin de Guer: Charles Guerlin de Guer, *Le parler populaire de la commune de Thaon (Calvados)*, Paris, 1901.

Hellquist: Elof Hellquist, *Svensk Etymologisk Ordbok*, 3rd edition, Lund, 1948.

Joret: Charles Joret, *Des caractères et de l'extension du patois normand*, Paris, 1883.

Joret, 1913: Charles Joret, *Les Noms de lieu d'origine non romane et la colonisation germanique et scandinave en Normandie*, Paris, 1913.

Kemna: K. Kemna, *Der Begriff "Schiff" im Französischen*, Marburg, 1901.

Kluge: Friedrich Kluge, *Etymologisches Wörterbuch der deutschen Sprache*, Berlin, 1951.

Littré: Émile Littré, *Dictionnaire de la langue française*, Paris, 1873.

Longnon: Auguste Longnon, *Les Noms de lieu de la France,* Paris, 1920-29.

Métivier: G. Métivier, *Dictionnaire franco-normand, ou recueil de mots particuliers au dialecte de Guernesey,* London-Edinburgh, 1870.

Moisy: Henri Moisy, *Dictionnaire du patois normand indiquant particulièrement tous les termes de ce patois en usage dans la région centrale de la Normandie,* Caen, 1887.

Nyrop: Kr. Nyrop, *Grammaire historique de la langue française,* I, Copenhagen, 1899.

Nyrop, *Wörter und Sachen:* Kr. Nyrop, "Ein vermeintliches Wikingerwort," *Wörter und Sachen,* VII (1921), 81-101.

OED: *A New English Dictionary on Historical Principles,* ed. James and H. Murray, Oxford, 1888-1933.

Pope: M. K. Pope, *From Latin to Modern French with Especial Consideration of Anglo-Norman,* Manchester, 1952.

Poppe: E. Poppe, *Der Wortschatz des Journal des Sieur de Gouberville in seinen Beziehungen zu den heutigen normannischen Mundarten,* Leipzig, 1936.

RDR: *Revue de dialectologie romane,* Brussels (later Hamburg), 1909-1915.

REW: W. Meyer-Lübke, *Romanisches Etymologisches Wörterbuch,* 3rd ed., Heidelberg, 1935.

RLiR: *Revue de linguistique romane,* Paris, 1925 ff.

RLR: *Revue des langues romanes,* Montpellier and Paris, 1870 ff.

Saggau: R. Saggau, *Die Benennungen der Schiffsteile und Schiffsgeräte im Neufranzösischen,* Kiel, 1905.

Sainéan, *Sources indigènes:* L. Sainéan, *Les Sources indigènes de l'étymologie française,* Volumes I-III, Paris, 1925-1930.

Sandahl: Bertil Sandahl, *Middle English Sea Terms. I. The Ship's Hull. Essays and Studies on English Language and Literature,* VIII, Upsala, 1951.

Sjögren: A. Sjögren, "Le Genre des mots d'emprunt norrois en normand," *Romania,* LIV (1928), 381-412.

Skautrup: Peter Skautrup, *Det Danske Sprogs Historie,* I, Copenhagen, 1944.

Thomas, *Mélanges:* Antoine Thomas, *Mélanges d'étymologie française,* 2nd ed., Paris, 1902.

Tobler: Adolf Tobler and Erhard Lommatzsch, *Altfranzösisches Wörterbuch*, Berlin, 1925-.

Valkhoff: Marius Valkhoff, *Les Mots français d'origine néerlandaise*, Amersfoort, 1931.

Vincent: A. Vincent, *Toponymie de la France*, Brussels, 1937.

ZFSL: *Zeitschrift für französische Sprache und Literatur*, Oppeln und Leipzig, 1879 ff.

ZRPh: *Zeitschrift für romanische Philologïe*, Leipzig, 1877 ff.

ABBREVIATIONS OF GRAMMATICAL TERMS, LANGUAGES, ETC.

acc.	accusative
adj.	adjective
adv.	adverb
AN	Anglo-Norman
AS	Anglo-Saxon
C.	Calvados
c.	century
ca.	circa
ch.	chapter
cf.	*confer* 'compare'
E.	Eure
ed.	edition by
ff.	and the following
Fr.	French
Gmc.	Germanic
Icel.	Icelandic (modern)
Lat.	Latin
LL	Low Latin of Normandy
M.	Manche
MFr.	Middle French
n.	neuter
N. Arch.	naval architecture
naut.	nautical
Norm.	Norman
Norw.	Norwegian
O.	Orne
ODan.	Old Danish
OE	Old English
OF	Old French
OIcel.	Old Icelandic

ON	Old Norse
ONorm.	Old Norman
OPic.	Old Picard
OSwed.	Old Swedish
p. pp.	page (s)
p. p.	past participle
pl.	plural
pl. name	place-name
PN	proper name
s.f.	feminine substantive
S.-I.	Seine-Inférieure (now Seine-Maritime)
s.m.	masculine substantive
s.n.	neuter substantive
s.v.	*sub voce* or *verbo* 'under the word'
Swed.	Swedish
tr.	translated by
v.	verse
v.i.	verb intransitive
VL	Vulgar Latin
v. tr.	verb transitive

PHONETIC SYMBOLS

The phonetic symbols used in this study are those of the International Phonetic Alphabet, with the following exceptions:

[č]   indicates the affricative sound, as in English *church*.

[ǧ]   indicates the affricative sound, as in English *judge*.

[ʒ]   indicates the velar fricative, as in Spanish *llegar*.

[ḳ]   indicates a palatalized sound, between [k] and [č].

[ǫ]   in phonetic transcriptions of French words is used to indicate the vowel in the word *bosse*.

[ọ]   is used to indicate the vowel in French *sot*.

[š]   is used for the hushing fricative in English *ash*.

[þ]   is used instead of [θ], as in English *think*.

[ž]   is used to indicate the hushing fricative of English *pleasure*.

[ ]   indicates a phonetic transcription.

>   denotes *has become*.

<   denotes *has been derived from*.

ˊ   in OIcel. words denotes a long vowel.

—   in ODan. words indicates a long vowel.

INTRODUCTION

As early as 1611, Cotgrave wrote that the word *haro* or *harol* was used in Normandy "by such as are outraged, or in some high degree wronged; therby seeming to implore th'aid of their Duke Rol. . . ." Similarly, Ménage had a fantastic explanation for the origin of the word *bigot* in the *Dictionnaire étymologique de la langue française*: "Rollon étant conseillé par les siens de baiser les piés à Charles, petit fils de Charles le Chauve, en reconnoissance de ce qu'il lui donnoit le Duché de Normandie et sa fille Gisle (sic) en mariage, refusa de la faire, disant en sa langue 'ne se bigot'; quasi, non per Deum. De quoi le Roi et les Courtisans s'étant moqués, lui donnèrent le soubriquet de Bigot; d'où vient que les Normans ont été appelés Bigots." Diderot, *Encyclopédie*, XXIII, 119 has an etymology similar to Cotgrave's. Louis Dubois, in his "Recherches sur l'étymologie et l'emploi des locutions et des mots qui se sont introduits ou conservés dans le département de l'Orne, et qui n'appartiennent pas à la langue française de nos jours", *Mémoires de l'Académie Celtique*, V (1810), 39-50, 173-180, was curious about the origin of Norman words, but contributed nothing of importance as far as etymologies are concerned. At approximately the same time when interest in place-names of Norse origin was growing in Normandy, certain Norman lexicographers began to be interested in the Scandinavian influence on the Norman vocabulary. Raynouard, in the *Journal des savans* (Paris, 1820), pp. 393 ff., had hinted at the possibility of Norse influence in Normandy. Unfortunately, some Norman lexicographers exaggerated the importance of the Norse contribution to the Norman vocabulary. This was the case in the work of Edouard Le Héricher, *Normandie scandinave* (Avranches, 1861) and in that of the Duméril brothers.[1] No really serious study of the Norse influence on Norman vocabulary was made. As a matter of fact, it was not until 1954 that a systematic study of Norman personal names of Scandinavian origin appeared.[2]

Auguste Jal, *Archéologie navale* (Paris, 1840) and *Glossaire nautique* (Paris, 1848) was aware that there was some Norse influence on French nautical terms, and Diez also suggested such an influence.[3] During the last three decades of the 19th century, various French and Norman words were traced to Norse by Sophus Bugge, Charles Joret and Antoine Thomas in articles appearing in *Romania*.[4] Joret was aware of the difficulty involved in ascribing a given Norman word to a particular Germanic language, in view of the fact that the Saxons had had important settlements in pre-viking Neustria.[5] A. Thomas also presented important material on Norse words in French in his works, *Essais de philologie française* (1897), *Mélanges d'étymologie française* (1902) and *Nouveaux Essais de philologie française* (1904). Thomas' etymologies are usually well founded; the excellence of the *Dictionnaire général* is, in a large measure, due to his collaboration.[6]

The appearance of the first fascicules of W. von Wartburg's *Französisches Etymologisches Wörterbuch* in 1928 was important for the student of French etymology. The author presented valuable material on the history and the geographical extension of each word; in many cases, it was shown that a given word existed only in Normandy and was absent from the patois of other areas of heavy Germanic influence, making Norse origin quite certain for the word in question. In the 3rd edition of the *Romanisches Etymologisches Wörterbuch,* Meyer-Lübke lists many Norse etymologies for French words, and also rejects many for phonetic or semantic reasons. He made use of articles in the philological journals to a greater extent than the patois dictionaries, and consequently the reader does not get the complete picture which he gets from the *FEW*.

One of the few works to treat the phonetic problems of Norse words in Norman is Anders Pedersen, "Nogle Normanniske Lydforhold", *Danske Studier*, 1911, pp. 85-98. Some good ideas are presented, but unfortunately the author did not expand the ideas presented in the article.[7] On the other hand, Albert Sjögren, "Le Genre des mots d'emprunt norrois en normand", *Romania* LIV (1928), 381-412 is a detailed study of one aspect of the Norse words in Norman. Writing in the *Revue internationale d'onomas-*

tique, IV (1952), 161-167, Pierre Fouché presented evidence to show that Norman place-names in *-beuf* and *-fleur* are not of Norse origin, because diphthongization had taken place long before the Viking settlement of Neustria.

A number of studies were made on the subject of French nautical terms, with some consideration of Norse influence on the vocabulary. H. Saggau's *Die Benennungen der Schiffsteile und Schiffsgeräte im Neufranzösischen* (Kiel, 1905); K. Kemna's *Der Begriff "Schiff" im Französischen* (Marburg, 1901) and W. Frahm's *Das Meer und die Seefahrt in der altfranzösischen Literatur* (Göttingen, 1914) included some Norse etymologies, but the material is not examined from the phonetic point of view. Some treatment of French words is found in H. Falk, "Altnordisches Seewesen", *Wörter und Sachen*, IV (1912), 1-122. Some of Falk's etymologies were criticized by K. Nyrop in "Et formentligt Viking-erord" in the *Aarbøger for nordisk Oldkyndighed og Historie*, 3rd ser., IX (Copenhagen, 1919), 1-34.[8]

Important contributions were made by Paul Barbier on the subject of fishes, nautical terms and other words in French and its dialects, in articles appearing in the *Revue des langues romanes, Zeitschrift für französische Sprache und Literatur, Romania, Revue de dialectologie romane* and *Revue de linguistique romane*, as well as in the series "Miscellanea Lexicographica" in the *Proceedings of the Leeds Philosophical Society*. W. von Wartburg called the latter series "un des apports les plus importants à la connaissance du lexique francais."[9] Barbier discovered a number of Scandinavian etymologies for Norman words, and was one of the few to question the alleged Anglo-Saxon influence on French, which few had ever seemed to doubt. He was extremely conscious of the importance of phonetic chronology as a means of determining the approximate date that a given Germanic word entered French. The results of Barbier's research have been one of our most important sources of information in the present study.

A few words should be said about the treatment of Norse words in French as presented in some of the best known histories of the French language. Ferdinand Brunot's *Histoire de la langue française* (Paris, 1924) I, 286-7 includes the incorrect statement that ONorm. *esneque* 'a type of ship' and ONorm. *brant* 'prow' are still part of the Norman patois, and that *drenc* is used in Normandy with the meaning 'boy', whereas the truth of the matter is that there was an ONorm. *drenc* with the meaning 'cable, rope' like nautical Fr. *dran* (from ON *dreng-r* 'boy, cable, rope'), but these words have never been attested in France with the meaning 'boy'. A similar statement is found in Nyrop, *Grammaire historique de la langue française*, I, 18. Brunot's statement that Fr. *bateau* is from Old Norse has been repeated by Marcel Cohen, *Histoire d'une langue: le français* (Paris, 1947), p. 69 and by Paul Lévy, *La Langue allemande en France* (Lyon-Paris, 1950), p. 37. Yet ON *bát-r* 'boat' was taken from Anglo-Saxon probably long after 900.

Whereas Anders Pedersen, *Danske Studier* (1911) pp. 85-98 concluded that there was no Norse influence on Norman pronunciation, others have sought to find evidence of Norse substratum in Normandy. Dauzat states in *Les Patois*, p. 143 that aspirate [h] has been retained in Norman in the regions where Norse colonization was strongest. In an earlier study in the *Revue de philologie française et de littérature*, XXXVIII (1926), 110, n. 4, Dauzat states that the Norsemen did not exert any appreciable influence on the Romance phonetics of Normandy, the colonists having brought no women with them. In the *Histoire de la langue française* (Paris, 1930), p. 80, Dauzat writes: "L'assourdissement des sonores . . . à la finale des mots romans (qu'on retrouve de nos jours dans certains patois normands, par exemple cauchois, particulièrement imprégnés de substrat norrois), est commun au français et au provençal". In "Le Substrat germanique dans l'évolution phonétique du français" in *Mélanges de linguistique et de philologie offerts à J. van Ginneken* (Paris, 1937), p. 267, Dauzat states that at Yport the word *piège* is pronounced with a voiceless final consonant due to the influence of either the Saxons or Norsemen who had once lived in the region. A year earlier, Walther von Wartburg came forth with a theory that the Scandinavians were in some way responsible for the non-palatalization of [k] in Normandy north of the Lisieux-Coutances-Évreux-Beauvais line. This hypothesis, which appeared in the *Zeitschrift für romanische Philologie*, LVI (1936), and was repeated in

Die Ausgliederung der romanischen Sprachräume (Bern, 1950),
was based on the fact that the distribution of Scandinavian place-
names in Normandy was most heavily represented in the same
area where non-palatalization was evident. W. von Wartburg's
theory was attacked by Albert Dauzat as "une théorie audacieuse"
in *Essais de géographie linguistique* (1938), p. 161. Dauzat
pointed out the fact that the area of non-palatalization extends
into Picardy, where there is no evidence of Viking influence. A
structural theory was presented by A.-G. Haudricourt and A.-G.
Juilland in the *Essai pour une histoire structurale du phonétisme
français* (Paris, 1949). Opposing W. von Wartburg's theory of
Scandinavian influence, these scholars explained the non-palatalization of [k] in Normandy and Picardy as directly connected
with the development of the diphthong [au].

Whereas some philologists exaggerated the importance of
Norse influence on French and especially Norman, others went
to the other extreme. J. Brüch, for example, writes in "Die bisherige Forschung über die germanischen Einflüsse auf die romanischen Sprachen", *RLR* II (1926) 25-98: "Da *gaber* verloren ist, so
sind die nautischen Ausdrücke *bittes, tillac, varangue, cingler*
'segeln' *vague* und *girouette* . . . die einzigen französischen Wörter altdänischen Ursprungs, die sich einer weiteren Verbreitung
noch heute erfreuen".[10] It would seem, then, that further study
of the Norse influence would be necessary to determine what
this influence was on the Norman and French vocabularies. It
is evident that a systematic study of the Norse element in French,
with consideration of the material available in Scandinavian and
English sources and with the probable phonology of Norse and
French of the late 9th century taken into account, has never been
made. In the pages which follow, we shall examine the phonology
of Old Danish, the phonology of 9th century French and the
French treatment of each of the Scandinavian phonemes, with
reference made to the English and Irish treatment of the same
phoneme when necessary. Finally a glossary of all French and
Norman words of probable Norse origin will be presented, with
the reasons for accepting or rejecting the etymology.

PART I

THE COMPARATIVE PHONOLOGY OF OLD
DANISH AND THE ROMANCE OF NORTH-
WESTERN FRANCE IN THE LATE
9th CENTURY

THE COMPARATIVE PHONOLOGY OF OLD DANISH AND THE ROMANCE OF NORTH-WESTERN FRANCE IN THE LATE 9th CENTURY

Old Danish

For an accurate picture of the phonological system of the language spoken by the Viking settlers of Neustria, we must examine the evidence supplied by the Danish runes of that period, Danish loans in other languages and chiefly Middle English, and Danish proper names quoted in foreign sources. By comparing this material with later stages of Old Danish, and taking into consideration any changes that may have taken place between 900 and the time of the introduction of Latin script into Denmark several centuries later, we should be able to obtain some idea of the phonological system of Old Danish in 900.

The following were the Old Danish consonants: [11]

	Labials	Apicals	Sibilants	Palatals	Velars
Plosives (voiced)	b- -bb-	d- -dd-			g -gg
(voiceless)	p- -pp-	t -tt-			k -kk
Spirants (voiced)	-t-	-ð-			ᴣ
(voiceless)	f-	þ	s -ss	χ	h
Laterals		l -ll			
Vibrants		r -rr		ʀ	
Nasals	m -mm	n -nn			ŋ
Semi-vowels	w			j	

Old Danish had the following vowels which could be either long or short:

i y u
e ø o
ę a ǫ

In addition, Old Danish had a series of nasal vowels, but, of these, the only one for which there was a special runic symbol was [ã]. It is also the only ODan. nasal vowel to be treated differently in Neustria from the oral vowels.

Old Danish had the following diphthongs in 900:

ai ǫu iū
ia io øy

The vowel [ǫ] resulting from u-mutation of [a] seems to have caused disagreement among linguists. Skautrup lists it as part of the phonology of Old Danish during the Viking period,[12] giving as examples wǫr (from earlier waruʀ) and mǫg 'son' from earlier magu. Skautrup says that this sound change took place in the 8th century, although it did not take place everywhere to the same extent. Björkman, in *Scandinavian Loan Words in Middle English*, p. 288, states that the regular ME representation of Scandinavian [ǫ] is [a], but he adds that it is impossible to decide whether this [a] rests on Scandinavian [a] or [ǫ], since in the East Scandinavian sources Primitive Norse [a] is frequently unchanged, while in Old West Scandinavian, [ǫ] is the regular sound.[13] In studying the same problem, Karl Luick, *Historische Grammatik der englischen Sprache*, I¹, 382, after stating that East Norse forms with [a] are partly the source of English words with [a] (where Old Icelandic had [ǫ]), suggests that perhaps Scandinavian [ǫ] was closer to OE and ME [a] than to OE and ME [o]. Carl Marstrander, *Bidrag til det norske Sprogs Historie i Irland*, p. 74, found that ON [ǫ] was regularly identified by the Irish with Irish [a], as for example in the proper name *Ascall* (< ON *Hǫskuld-r*). Marstrander concludes that the difference between [a] and the u-mutated variation of that sound must not have been very great during the first two centuries of the Viking period, since the Irish treated both [a] and [ǫ] as the same sound, or at least identified them both with Irish [a]. Irish *rang-brised*, ME *wranga* and Fr. *varangue* are all related to OIcel. *rǫng* 'rib in a ship'. It would seem then that the vowel of the ON etymon must have been [a] at the time the words were adopted.

Another characteristic of Old Danish was the retention of [w] + consonant in initial position, where Old Icelandic and Old Norwegian had lost [w]. Cf. ME *wranga* and Fr. *varangue,* from ODan. *°wrang,* as opposed to OIcel. *rǫng.*

The Phonology of Northern French in the Late 9th Century

In order to obtain as accurate a picture as possible of the phonology of the Romance dialect encountered by the Viking settlers of Neustria, we can use the evidence offered by the *Cantilène de Ste. Eulalie.* Probably composed ca. 880 in Picardy, it represents fairly well the language spoken in pre-viking Normandy, granting that there was no appreciable difference linguistically in those two regions of France before the early 10th century. The *Homélie sur le prophète Jonas* has also been consulted; such works as the *Passion du Christ* and the *Vie de Saint Léger* contain too many Provençal forms to be of any value for our present purposes. The *Serments de Strasbourg* offer too controversial a picture of some not perfectly identified form of 9th century French to be of any direct value in the present research.

[p] and [b]

The type of Romance under discussion must have had two bilabial phonemes [p] and [b] well attested word and syllable initially, chiefly as the normal outcomes of the corresponding phonemes of Latin, and, chiefly for [b], of Frankish: cf. *buona, pulcella* (*Eulalie,* 1) and the many French words and names of Frankish origin with initial [b] which are centuries older than the *Eulalie,* although not attested in that work: however, cf. *baron* in the *Vie de Saint Léger,* a 10th century work (Bloch, s.v. *baron*). Intervocalic [p] as the reflex of an older geminate occurs in the Latin form *opidum* in an 8th century document.[14] (cf. Pope, p. 147). The form *colomb* (*Eulalie,* 25) ends in [p], the reflex of the older [b] (cf. Pope, p. 98).

Intervocalic *b* was probably rare, occurring in *abes* 'abbé' (< *abbas*) (cf. Pope, p. 147).

[f] and [v]

Romance [f] (< Latin [f]) occurred word and syllable initially; cf. *fut* (*Eulalie,* 1). Another origin of Romance initial [f] was as a replacement of Frankish [χ], as in OF *frime* (< *°hrim*) (Pope, p. 227). Intervocalic [f] is attested in *defendut* (*Jonas,* cf. Bartsch, p. 7, 1. 26) and also in words in which Latin had -*ff*-.

[v] occurred word and syllable initially, from an earlier Lat. u-: cf. *voldrent, servir* (*Eulalie,* 3, 4). [v] occurred intervocalically mainly as the reflex of Lat. -*p*-, -*b*- and -*u*- (cf. Pope, pp. 256, 258 and 260).

[t] and [d]

The Romance dialect we are considering must have had two occlusive phonemes [t] and [d] attested word and syllable initially, chiefly as the normal outcomes of the corresponding phonemes of Latin; cf. *tuit* (*Eulalie,* 26), *deo* (*Eulalie,* 3) and *sostendreiet* (*Eulalie,* 16). Intervocalic [t] as the reflex of an older geminate is probably in the form *getterent* (*Eulalie,* 19) in spite of the spelling. Intervocalic [d] as the reflex of the geminate was certainly rare if it did exist. Final [t] was found as the reflex of Lat. [t] and Lat. [d] become final; cf. [tart] (< *tardum*), (Pope, p. 261), *argent* (*Eulalie,* 7), and *fut* (*Eulalie,* 1).

[ð]

The type of Romance under discussion must have had the phoneme [ð] attested intervocalically as the reflex of Lat. -*t*- and -*d*-: cf. *spede* (*Eulalie,* 22) and *empedementz* (*Eulalie,* 16). [þ] was probably attested as a variant of [ð] in final position (cf. Pope, p. 140). In the forms *perdesse* and *arde,* [þ] had already begun to be effaced before homophonous consonants (cf. Pope, p. 140), but in *sostendreiet* (*Eulalie*, 16) |þ] is kept. (Cf. Pope, p. 346).

[s] and [z]

[s] was attested word and syllable initially as the normal outcome of the corresponding phoneme in Latin; cf. *servir* (*Eulalie*, 4). Intervocalic -*s*- was the outcome of Latin -*ss*-; cf. *perdesse* (*Eulalie*, 17). Romance [-*z*-] was the normal reflex of Latin -*s*-: cf. *kose* (*Eulalie*, 23). Romance -*s* is attested: *corps* (*Eulalie*, 2), *mals* (*Eulalie*, 5), etc. Cf. Pope, pp. 137–138.

[ts] and [dz]

The phoneme [ts] must have occurred in initial position as the normal outcome of Lat. *ci*- and *ce*-: cf. *celle* (*Eulalie*, 23). For [-ts-] in intervocalic position, cf. the forms cited by Pope, p. 276, *supersticiosos* and *superstitiones* in the *Glossary of Reichenau,* and cf. also *manatce* (*Eulalie*, 8; Pope, p. 279). The phoneme [dz] was found only intervocalically and was probably rare; cf. *bellezour* in *Eulalie*, 2, and the numerals *unze, doze* and *treze* (cf. Pope, p. 93). In final position, only [ts] occurred, being written -*z*: cf. *paramenz* (*Eulalie*, 7; cf. Pope, p. 276).

[č] and [ğ]

The type of Romance under discussion did not palatalize [k] and [g] initial followed by [a]; cf. *cosa* (*Eulalie*, 8). Coastal Normandy must have also retained [k] intervocalically; in the Norman-Picard area, [č] was the normal outcome of initial [k] plus Lat. *e, i,* syllable initial and intervocalic [kj] and syllable initial [tj]: cf. *avanchier, princhier, pieche, blieche* in the writings of Renclus de Moiliens (Pope, p. 487). Cf. also the forms *Franche, fache, fach* (< *franciam, faciam, facio*) (Pope, p. 130).

[ğ] word and syllable initial must have been the normal outcome of Lat. *ia* and *di*-: cf. *getterent* (*Eulalie*, 19). Cf. also Pope, p. 131. Intervocalic [ğ] must have existed as the outcome of yod in syllable initial position; cf. *rouge* (< *rubeum*) etc. (Pope, p. 129).

[k] and [g]

There must have been two stops [k] and [g] word and syllable initially, the normal outcome of the corresponding phonemes of Latin; cf. *corps, eskoltet, grand* (*Eulalie*, 2, 5, 18). Final [k] existed as the reflex of an older geminate in forms such as *sec* (< *siccum*) (Pope, p. 269), and as the reflex of older [g] not found in word final position: cf. *lonc* (< *longum*, Pope, p. 98).

Latin [kw] word initially must have simplified to [k] before [e] and [i] before the composition of the *Eulalie*: cf. *chi, Eulalie*, 6 (Pope, p. 93). [kw] initial before [a] must have persisted until a later period, to judge from the late survival of the [w] in Anglo-Norman (Pope, p. 449). Initial [gw] from Germanic initial [w] had not yet simplified to [g] at the time of composition of *Eulalie;* this is shown by words such as *guard* introduced into England with the [w]. Pope, p. 93, states that [gw] simplified to [g] before the late 12th century.

[j]

The type of Romance under discussion must have had a phoneme [j] which was the outcome of intervocalic Lat. [k] and [g]: cf. *pleier* (*Eulalie*, 9) from Lat. *plicare; raneiet* (*Eulalie*, 6) from Lat. *reneget*. Cf. also the forms *coist* (*Eulalie*, 20) from Lat. *coxit* and *laist* (*Eulalie*, 28) from Lat. *laxit*. Cf. also Pope, pp. 133, 136-137.

[w]

[w] must have existed initially in stretches of Northern and Western France. The phoneme, which was of Frankish origin, had passed to [gw] elsewhere in France (cf. Pope, pp. 227, 228 and 487). In Neustria, the coastal region retained [w] initially in words of Frankish origin; this phoneme later passed to [v], which is still common today in coastal Normandy (cf.

the family name *Vautier* corresponding to *Gautier*.) In the part
of Neustria adjacent to the Central French area, [w] must
have passed to [gw] (perhaps as early as the 7th century; cf.
Pope, p. 78), and this passed to [g] before the late 12th century (Pope, p. 93).

Gallo-Roman intervocalic [w] shifted to [v] if it persisted
in intervocalic position into Early Old French (i.e. roughly from
the middle of the 9th century to the end of the 11th) (Pope,
p. 93). There is no example of -*v*- (< Gmc. [-w-]) in *Eulalie*,
but cf. the form *avardevet*, a verb-form from Germanic (cf.
regarder) in the *Fragment d'une homélie sur le prophète Jonas*,
line 22, in Bartsch, *Chrestomathie*, p. 6. It is quite possible that
the change had already taken place in the Romance under discussion.

[l]

The dialect we are examining must have had [l] in all
positions: cf. *pulcella, Eulalia, bel, bellezour, voldrent, li, diaule*,
etc. (*Eulalie*, 1-4). In syllable final, e.g. in *bel*, the language had
dark [l], which later became [u]. The use of *l* in the orthography
of the *Eulalie* would seem to indicate that vocalization had not
yet taken place, although an isolated spelling from 832, *Caus
dou Pont*, shows that vocalization was in process elsewhere in
France (cf. Pope, p. 155).

Palatal [l]

The dialect under discussion must have had a palatal [l]
in intervocalic and final position. This phoneme had various
origins, including [l] followed by a yod, as in *filia* > [*filja] >
[*fil'ə]; or [ll] followed by a yod: cf. *allium* > *ail* (Pope, p. 131);
another source of palatal [l] was the development of [kl] and
[gl]: cf. *pariculum* > *pareclu* > *pareil* (Pope, p. 133). Cf. the
form *conselliers* (*Eulalie*, 5).

[r] and [rr]

There must have been a phoneme [r] in all positions as the normal outcome of Lat. [r]. There was a phoneme [rr] only in intervocalic position, as the normal development of Lat. [rr] or from other sources, such as Gallo-Roman [-ðr-]: cf. *verre* < *veiðre* < *vitrum* (cf. Pope, p. 149). Pope, p. 147, states that all the double consonants that were in use in Late Latin and all those formed by assimilation were reduced to single consonants except [rr] in intervocalic position, and [rr] intervocalic was simplified to [r] before the end of Middle French, usually with compensatory vowel lengthening. Martinet states that the traditional opposition was probably first affected in northern central France when in the 16th century *-r-* was shifted to [z].[15]

In *Eulalie* there appears to be no example of *-rr-*, but [r] occurs in various positions: *auret, corps, bellezour* (*Eulalie*, 2) and *raneiet* (*Eulalie*, 6). In initial position *r* may have had the value of [rr], as is the case in Castilian Spanish today.

[m], [n] and [ñ]

The phonemes [m], [n] and [ñ] were distinct in all positions except word and syllable final. [ŋ] occurred only as a variant of the nasal archiphoneme in syllable final.

[m] was the normal outcome of Lat. [m] except in syllable final position, and of certain Gallo-Roman consonant groups, such as *mn, nm* and *mb* (cf. Pope, p. 148). [n] was the normal outcome of Latin [n], and of all nasal phonemes in syllable final. [ñ] developed from Lat. [gn] (Pope, p. 133), as in Latin *agnellum* > OF *agnel*. For examples of the nasal phonemes in *Eulalie*, cf. *buona, anima, non, degnet* (*Eulalie*, 1, 2, 9, 26).

[h]

The phoneme [h] existed in initial position in the many words of Frankish origin beginning with that sound. In Latin words, [h] had already disappeared from the sound system in Late Latin (Pope, p. 15). There are no examples of [h] in the *Cantilène de Ste Eulalie.*

STRESSED VOWELS

[a] < Lat. *a* in checked syllables: *grand* (*Eulalie*, 18).

[ę] < VL ę in checked syllables: *auret, bellezour* (*Eulalie*, 2; cf. Pope, p. 278).

[ẹ] < VL ẹ in checked syllables: *perdesse* (*Eulalie*, 17; cf. Pope, p. 383).

[e] a phoneme distinguished originally by length, with timbre varying through the centuries < Lat. *a* in open syllables: cf. *presentede* (< Lat. *presentata*) (*Eulalie*, 11).

[i] in most cases from Lat. ī: *chi* (*Eulalie*, 6) < Latin *qui*.

[ǫ] < VL ǫ in checked syllables: cf. *corps* (*Eulalie*, 2).

[ọ] < VL ọ in checked syllables: cf. *nom* (*Eulalie*, 14). During the period which interests us, [ọ] must have been part of the pattern, later passing to [u] in the course of the 11th and 12th centuries (Pope, p. 90).

[o] < Latin *au*: cf. *cose* (*Eulalie*, 9). This vowel may have had the same degree of aperture as [ǫ] < Vulgar Latin [ǫ] (cf. Pope, p. 128).

[u] was mainly the outcome of Lat. ū, and was passing to [y]: cf. *figure* (*Eulalie*, 25).

[íe] < VL e in open syllables: cf. *ciel* (*Eulalie*, 6) (Cf. also Pope, p. 192).

[ei] < VL ę in open syllables: cf. *rex* (*Eulalie*, 12) with a Latin spelling for [réis] (Ewert, p. 110).

[úo]< VL ǫ in open syllables: cf. *buona* (*Eulalie*, 1).

[ọu]< VL ọ in open syllables: cf: *bellezour, soure, souue* (*Eulalie*, 2, 12, 29); cf. also Pope, p. 105. Both this diphthong and [ọ] will pass to [u] in Norman French as [u] passes to [y]. (Cf. also Pope, p. 90).

[au] from an earlier [aβ] may have been in existence at this time: cf. *auret* (*Eulalie*, 2). [au] from [al] must have been impending (Pope, p. 155).

[ái]< Lat. *a* in open syllable before a nasal, and from *a* plus *c*: cf. *faire, maent, laist* (*Eulalie*, 4, 6, 28).

[ói]< Lat. *o* plus *c*: cf. *coist* (*Eulalie*, 20).

[úi]< Lat. *u* plus *c* must have been part of the phonology; Lat. *punctura* must have been at the stage °*puinture* (cf. Pope, p. 181). The form *fuiet* (*Eulalie*, 14) seems to contain this diphthong.

There seems to be no evidence of nasal vowels in the *Cantilène de Sainte Eulalie.*[16]

[ə]

[ə] was found in unstressed posttonic position (< Latin *a*). Final [ə]< Lat. *e, i, o, u* had already been effaced during the 8th and 9th centuries (Pope, p. 79; cf. also pp. 112, 113). Examples of [ə]< Lat. *a* are the following: *buona, pulcella* (*Eulalie, 1*).

The unstressed pretonic vowels will not be treated here since they have no bearing on the research.

The Romance Treatment of the Old Danish Linguistic Material

The Romance Treatment of the Old Danish Consonants.[17]

[b-]

ODan. [b-] was equated with Romance [b-], attested only word initially: ON *biti* 'cross-beam'> Fr. *bitte* 'bollard'; ON *bekk-r* 'brook'> Norm. *-bec* (in pl. names, *Caudebec*, etc.)

[-bb-]

ODan. [-bb-] seems to have been treated as Romance [-b-]. The geminate [-bb-] did not survive at this time in Neustria:[18] ON *gabba* 'to mock'> OF *gaber* 'to mock'.

[d]

Initially and after [n], the phoneme [d] was treated as OF [d]: ON *dreng-r* 'thick rope'> OF *drenc*, Fr. *dran* 'truss, rope';

ON *tundr* 'tinder'> Norm. *tondre* 'rotten wood used as fuel'. In
the Norm. forms from ON *sild* 'herring', the final consonant
was unvoiced, as were all voiced plosives and fricatives brought
into final position. Cf. Lat. *perdo*> OF *pert,* Lat. *lungum*>
OF *lonc,* Lat. *corvum*> OF *corp.*[19] This accounts for ONorm.
selletan 'herring', which was probably based on an original
ONorm. *°silt* + a suffix. In other forms of the word, the [-d]
was lost before the suffixes were added: OF *scellan,* Pic. *célan,*
Fr. *célerin.* For ONorm. *tialz* 'tent for ships not in use', we may
assume that ON *tjald* 'tent on ships esp. when in harbor' was
pronounced by the Romance speakers as *°tialt,* and that *tialz*
is originally the acc. pl. and nom. sing. form.

[-dd]

There are no reliable examples of ODan. [-dd] in Norse
loan words in French. Cf. the Glossary, §283.

[g] and [ʒ]

The Romance speakers of Normandy treated ODan. [g]
as their native [g]: ON *gabba* 'to mock'> ONorm. *gaber* 'to
mock'; ON *Gunnur*> ONorm. *Gunnor, Gonnor* (J. A. des
Gautries, 101-2). Intervocalically, ODan. [ʒ] seems to have
been treated as OF [g] in the ONorm. name *Stigand, Estigandus,*
etc. from ON *Stigand-r,* and the ONorm. place-name *Agevilla,*
Aguevilla, now *Acqueville,* M. from ODan. *Agi* (J. A. des Gautries, pp. 315-7, 375). In some cases, the voiced spirant must have
been lost very early, as in Fr. *vibord* 'sheer-strake' (< ON *vigi*
'bulwarks of ship' + ON *bord*), and Fr. *touer* 'to tow' from
ON *toga* 'to tow'. In final position, the ON sound was treated
as OF [k]; thus ON *Geirlaug*> ONorm. *Gerloc.* If the word has
survived, the final consonant is missing; ON *trog* 'trough'>
Norm. *tro* 'trough'. Fr. *vague* 'wave', first attested as ONorm.
wages 'waves' must have come from an ON plural, rather than
from ON *vág-r* itself; otherwise we should have expected a form
°vak. In Normandy we find traces of an unvoicing of intervocalic
[g]: ON *hrogn,* ODan. *rogn* 'roe'> Norm., Fr. *rogue,* Norm.
roque; Helgavilla (from ON *Helgi* + *villa*)> *Heuqueville,* E.

but cf. *Heugueville*, M. attested in 1115 as *Helgevilla* (J. A. des Gautries, pp. 396-7). A most unusual development seems to be that of the Norman place-name *Tourgéville* from *Torgisvilla* (< ON *þorgisl* + *villa*), the palatalization of [g] to [ǧ] having taken place in French by the 6th or 7th centuries.[20] However, the *OED* traces Fr. *targe* 'shield' to ON *targa* 'small round shield' (cf. *OED*, s.v. *target*) although Fr. *targe* must be older than the 10th century. Also difficult to explain is the development of ON *Holmgeirr* + *villa* to the Norman place-name *Hougerville* (J. A. des Gautries, p. 399).

[-gg]

ODan. [-gg] must have been treated as [g] by the Romance speakers: ON *hǫggva* 'to hew'> Norm. *haguer* 'to hew'; ON *Skeggi* is only attested in Normandy with [k], in the place-names *Eskeketot* and *Schechevilla*, now *Ecuquetot* and *St-Vaast-d'Equiqueville* respectively (J. Adigard des Gautries, pp. 413-4).

[ŋ]

Since [ŋ] did not occur in final position in 10th century French, it automatically became [nk], as in native Gallo-Roman words; cf. OF *lonc* from Lat. *longum*. ON *dreng-r* 'thick rope'> ONorm. *drenc;* ON *streng-r* 'string, rope'> ONorm. *estrenc* 'rope'. In some words, the phoneme [ŋ] was retained, by the addition of a final vowel: ODan. *°karling*, ON *kerling*> OF *carlingue* 'keelson'; ODan. *vrang* (cf. OIcel. *rǫng* 'piece of curved wood in a boat')> Fr. *varangue* 'floor timber'. Cf. also ON *Svarting-r* + *villa*> Norm. *Sortinvilla*, ca. 1062> *Surtainville*, M. (J .A. des Gautries, p. 418.) The fact that *dreng-r* also meant 'boy' and that *kerling* also meant 'woman' must have influenced the gender of the words *drenc* and *carlingue* in French, even though the words are attested in France only in their nautical meanings.[21]

[p]

The ODan. voiceless labial [p] was treated as OF [p], as in the following examples: ON *skipari* 'seaman'> ONorm. *es-*

kipre, OF *eschipre* 'seaman'; ODan. *Api* + *villa*> *Appa villa*>
Appeville, S.-I. (J. A. des Gautries, p. 377); ON *skipa* 'to man',
'to fit up'> OF *eschiper* 'to sail'> Fr. *équiper* 'to equip'. A
Frankish *°skipjan* would have developed as *°hapja*> *hache*
'axe' and would have given a Fr. verb in *-ir,* as *honnir, déguerpir,*
etc.

[pp]

There are few reliable examples of ODan. [pp] in French
or Norman. Perhaps Norm. *Cappetot,* S.-I. contains the ON
name *Kappi* (J. A. des Gautries, pp. 453-4).

[t]

ODan. [t] was regularly treated as OF [t]: ON *topt* 'homestead'> Norm. *-tot* (in place-names); ON *Ketill* + *villa*>
Ketelville> *Quetteville,* C. and M. (J. A. des Gautries, pp. 404-5);
ON *biti* 'cross-beam'> Fr. *bitte* 'bollard'; ON *klút-r*> OF *clut*
'rag'.

[tt]

ON *baratta* 'contest, fight, battle'> OF *barate* 'confusion,
agitation'.

[k] and [kk]

In all positions, ODan. [k] and [kk] were treated as OF
[k]: ODan. *Kati* + *villa*> *Catevilla, Catavilla,* now *Catteville*
(J. A. des Gautries, p. 117); ON *flikki* 'flitch'> Norm. *flique*
'flitch of bacon'; ON *bekk-r*> Norm. *bec* 'brook'; ON *snekkja,*
ODan. *°snekkia*> ONorm. *esneque* 'type of ship'[22] The Central
French palatalization of [k] must have still been in progress
when some Norman words of ON origin reached Paris; Norm.
flique> OF *fliche,* Fr. *flèche*; ONorm. *esneque*> OF *esneche.*
Cf. also ON *virki* 'fortress'> *Wirchia*> (*La*) *Guerche* (cf. Glossary §178). It is not usually stated that this palatalization was
still going on in Central French after 900. A more unusual example is the development of ON *Knapi* + *villa* into Norm.

Chenappeville as well as *Canappeville* and *Canapville* (for the forms cf. J. A. des Gautries 406). The name was attested in 1196 as *Kenapevilla* and *Canapevilla*.

[β]

The ODan. voiced labial spirant [β] was treated as [v] by the Romance speakers of Normandy. ON *stafn* 'stem of ship'> Fr. *étrave* 'stem-post'; ON *háf-r* + *net* 'net'> Fr. *havenet* 'shrimp net'. Another development was that of ON *stafn* into OF *estable*, *étable* 'stem-post'; cf. the development of ODan. °*hafn* (OIcel. *hǫfn* 'port') into OF *hable, havle,* ONorm. *havene,* Fr. *havre* 'port'. Meyer-Lübke's derivation of Guernsey *skauir* 'to eat' from ODan. *skaffe* is phonetically impossible,[23] as is also Gamillscheg's derivation of OF *rebiffer* from ON *bifa*.[24] Fr. *hauban*, OF *hobent* 'shroud' must be from ODan. °*hafuð-benda* (cf. OIcel. *hǫfuð-benda* 'shroud'). With early reduction of intervocalic [β], the next stage must have been °*hauðbent*, with consequent reduction of the consonant cluster to [b], giving °*haubent, hobent.* Cf. also the development of ON *Svarthǫfði, Svarthǫfuð* + *villa* to the ONorm. place-name *Sortoovilla,* now *Surtauville,* E., through a probable intermediate stage °*Sortoudvilla* (cf. J. A. des Gautries, 417-8).

[ð]

The ODan. voiced spirant [ð] must have been equated with OF [ð] which was certainly still found in intervocalic position in Normandy after the Viking settlement took place.[25] However in all attested forms of ONorm. words and names, the [ð] had already disappeared: ON *Sumarliði* + *villa* developed into *Summerleevilla,* attested ca. 1210 (cf. J. A. des Gautries, p. 417); ON *greiða* 'to unravel'> OF *gréer* 'to rig'; ON *braeða* 'to tar' > Fr. *brayer* 'to tar'; ON *støðing-r* 'studding sail'> ONorm. *estoinc.* In the ON name *þorfrøðr,* [ð] was not intervocalic, but in Normandy it became intervocalic in the form *Turfredus* and in the place-name *Turfredivilla* attested in 1068, now *Touffréville.* Cf. also the form *Turfretvilla* attested ca. 1040, now *Touffreville-la-Corbeline.*[26] In Normandy, [þ] was a variant of [ð] occurring in final position; thus ON words ending in [ð] were pronounced by the Romance speakers with [þ]. The later development of this Romance [þ] to |t| is unusual and has not been explained. Perhaps the spelling -t represented [þ]; cf. *sostendreiet* in *Eulalie* where t represents [þ] (cf. Pope, pp. 142-3; 346). ON *floð* 'flood'> Fr. *flot* 'wave'; ON *Smið-r* + *villa*> *Smit villa, Esmitvilla*, now *Emainville, Emiéville*, respectively.[27] Norm. *tierre* 'tether' must be from an ODan. *°tiuðr* (cf. OIcel. *tjóðr*). The earliest Norman form must have been *°tiedre*, developing into *tierre*, as *fradre*, probably pronounced [freðrə] in the *Oaths of Strasbourg* developed into *frère*. Cf. §230 below. Thus OF *edre* 'eider' does not date from the Viking settlement of Normandy (cf. §105, §299). For the early loss of [ð] in consonant clusters, cf. ONorm. *wirewite* from ON *veðr-viti* 'weather-vane', Fr. *hauban* 'shroud' from ODan. *°hafuð-benda*, ON *hǫfuð-benda*, and the place-name *Surtauville*, older *Sortoovilla* from ON *Svarthǫfuð* + *villa* (J. A. des Gautries, pp. 417-8). Forms such as Norm. *bruman* 'bridegroom' and the place-name *Flottemanville* are not from OIcel. forms in *mað-r*, but from ODan. forms in *mann*-R.[28]

[f]

ODan. [f] was treated as Romance [f] by the inhabitants of tenth-century Normandy. ON *fest-r* 'rope'> OF *feste* 'mooring cable'; ODan. *flundra* (cf. OIcel. *flyðra*) 'flounder'> Norm. *flondre* 'flounder'; ON *flana* 'to run about'> Fr. *flâner* 'to lounge about'.

[þ]

Although there was a voiceless spirant [þ] in late 9th century French, it was just a word final variant of [ð] and did not occur initially. The Romance speakers treated ON [þ] as [t]: ON *þang* 'sea-weed'> Norm. *tangon* 'sea-weed'; ON *þorlák-r* + *villa*> *Torlachvilla*> *Tourlaville*, M. (J. A. des Gautries, p. 429). Evidence that [þ] did not occur in initial position in Old French is given by the Norman treatment of English names of ON origin in the Domesday Book; for example, *Thorganby* appears as *Turgrimbi* and *Torgrembi*.[29] The spelling *th* in early Norman documents is used for both [t] and [þ]; *Théville* was attested as *Villa Teth* and *Tedvilla* in early documents.[30] *Tonneville* (from ODan. *Tummi, Tommi + villa*) was attested as *Thomevilla* in 1238; another locality from the same ODan. name was attested as *Tummavilla* in 1080 (J. A. des Gautries, p. 422).

[s]

ODan. [s] was regularly treated as Romance [s] in Normandy: ON *Sveinn* was attested as *Svenus* (J. A. des Gautries, p. 145); ON *sigla* 'to sail'> ONorm. *sigler* 'to sail'; ON *rás* 'course, channel'> Fr. *rás* 'strait, violent current'. The initial on-glide which developed in Late Latin before word initial pre-consonant [s] must have been in use in 10th century Normandy, although it was not always represented graphically. It was with the 12th century that prothetic [e] became a fixed integral part of the word.[31] Thus ON *Stigand-r* appears in Normandy as *Stigand* and *Estigand* (J. A. des Gautries, p. 249); ON *Smið-r + villa* appears as *Smit villa* and *Esmitvilla* (idem, p. 414). Words of the common vocabulary are not attested early enough to appear without prothetic [e]: ON *skaut* 'corner of a sail'> ONorm. *escote*, Fr. *écoute* 'sheet of sail'; ON *snekkja* > ONorm. *esneque*. A curious development is that of ON *Ásulf-r, Ōsulf-r + villa* into the Norman place-names *Auzouville, Ozeville, Ozouville*; cf. also *Le Mesnil-Auzouf* and *Champosoult* (*Campus Osulfi* ca. 1200). Cf. J. A. des Gautries, pp. 387-9. The [z] in the modern forms instead of [s] is difficult to explain; unfortunately there are no reliable examples of Norman or French words derived from ON forms with [-s-].[32] It would be hazardous to expect voicing of [-s-] in Normandy after 900, unless a parallel with the voicing of [-k-] to [-g-] is seen, the latter having taken place sporadically in Normandy.[33] It is likely too that the influence of orthography played a role since the modern names from *Ásulf-r* all have [-z-]. Cf. also *écraser* in the Glossary, §250.

[h]

It is quite certain that [h] existed in initial position followed by a vowel in the Romance of Neustria at the time of the Viking settlement; the heavy Germanic influence for several centuries before 900 must have contributed to perpetuate the existence of the phoneme. Thus ON [h] must have been equated with the already existent [h] of West Germanic origin. Whether the Scandinavian influence was responsible for the survival of [h] today in parts of Normandy has been disputed. Among the many examples of French words of ON origin with [h-] are: Fr. *homard*, ONorm. *houmar* < ON *humar-r* 'lobster'; Fr. *hune* 'top' < ON *hún-n* 'knob at top of mast-head'; and Fr. *hauban* 'shroud' < ODan. **hafuð-benda* (cf. OIcel. *hǫfuð-benda*) 'shroud'. In some localities in Normandy, an initial [r-] corresponding to [h-] is found: Norm. *rarné*, Fr. *harnais* 'harness' < ON **herr-nest* 'army provisions'; Norm. *ravenet*, Fr. *havenet* 'net' < ON **háfr-net* 'net'.[34] Already in the 9th century, [h] was being effaced in Denmark in the combinations [hr-], [hn-] and [hl-], a change which did not take place until the 11th century in Sweden and Norway. Norman words show the tendency to have initial [r-] rather than [hr-], probably an indication of stronger Danish influence than Norwegian: ODan. **rogn* (cf. OIcel. *hrogn* 'roe') > Fr. *rogue* 'roe'; ODan. *Rolf* (OIcel. *Hrolf-r*) > Norm. **Rol* (cf. Lat. *Rollo*) > Norm. *Rou*; ON *Hnakki* > *Nacqueville*. The replacing of [hr-] by [fr-] was no longer possible in 900; Fr. *frimas* could not be from ON *hrím* 'hoarfrost', as stated in the older etymological dictionaries.

[ç]

In addition to [h] which before a vowel was probably an aspirate as in Modern Danish, Old Danish had a voiceless spirant [ç] before consonantal [j] and [w]. ODan. [ç] must have been equated with OF [ǧ], the closest OF sound in that position. Thus ON **hjálm* 'rudder' became ONorm. **jalme*, OF *jaume* 'rudder'. Cf. Eng. *huge* with [hjudž] becoming [çudž], and also the development of ON [ç] to [š] in the Shetland

Norn: *Hjaltland*> *Shetland;* ON *hjarri* 'hinge'> Shetland Norn *sjarl-pin, sjarri-pin*.[35]

[l]

ODan. [l] was treated as Romance [l]: ON *sigla* 'to sail'> ONorm. *sigler* 'to sail'; ON *lund-r* 'grove'> Norm. *Londe,* a place-name; ON *hrossval-r*> OF *rohal* 'walrus'. In late 9th century Neustria there were various [l] sounds depending upon position in the word.[36] A velarized lateral [l] was used in the Romance of Neustria when that phoneme was pre-consonantal, and became vocalized to [u], a process which probably had its beginnings in the 9th century (Cf. Pope, p. 155). ON words appear in Normandy in their oldest forms with [l], but if the word has survived, pre-consonantal [l] has become vocalized: ON *kald-r kot* 'cold hut'> ONorm. *Caldecote*> *Caudecote*; ON *holmi* 'islet' appears in the name *Torhulmus, Turhulm* in the 11th century (J. A. des Gautries, pp. 422-3), and also as *-homme* in Norm. place-names. In Norm. *vamôque* (cf. OSwed. *valmoghe*) 'poppy', the [l] must have been lost very early, as was the case in *-homme,* whereas in Guernsey *houmet* 'presqu'île, pâturage assis sur l'eau' the [l] of ON *holmi* has been vocalized.[37] A final consonant after [l] tended to drop since that combination was not part of the phonology of the Romance dialect of the region: ON *elg-r*> ONorm. *hele* 'elk'; ON *Hrolf-r*>ONorm. *°Rol* > *Rou*; ODan. *°helm* 'rudder'> ONorm. *hel* 'rudder'. The coalescence of [l] and a following [j] in ON *þilja* 'plank, deck' and ON *Wilhjalm* must have been treated as the native Romance palatal lateral [l] in the contemporary form of Lat. *filia,* for example; thus the ON words appear in French as *tille* 'cuddy' and *Guillaume* respectively.[38] For the palatalization in Fr. *quille* 'keel' see Glossary §44, and *FEW,* II, 726. ON *°skriðla* 'to slide' (cf. Swed. dial. *skrilla*) must have been taken into Romance as *°escriðler* at the time when West Gmc. *Hruodland* was OF [roðlant]. ONorm. *escriler* is the normal outcome, but forms such as *écriller* and *égriller* 'to slide' are difficult to explain. Similarly, OF *guildrou* is the normal development of ON *kveldulf-r,* but the later stage *guilledou* in "courir le guilledou" is unusual. ON *þorgisl* appeared in Normandy without *l*, [-sl] being an unfamiliar final consonant cluster for the Romance speakers: *Turgis, Torguis*, etc. (J. A. des Gautries, p. 159).

[ll]

There was probably no distinction between [l] and [ll] in the Romance of Neustria ca. 900, and consequently ODan. [ll] must have been treated as Romance [l]. The spellings of ONorm. names are not always consistent as to the use of *l* or *ll*. ON *Bolli* + *villa* appears as *Bollivilla* as well as *Bolevilla* (J. A. des Gautries, p. 390). However the early forms of some Norm. place-names are surprisingly close to the ON etymon, in having one *l* like the ON name: cf. ON *Kali*, ONorm. *Caletot;* ON *Koli*, ONorm. *Colebosc, Coletot, Colevilla, Colivilla, Colemaisnillum, Colemare, Colewilla;* ON *Múli*, ONorm. *Mulevilla;* ON *Skúli*, ONorm. *Esculetot;* ODan. *Stáli*, ONorm. *Stalavilla*.[39] It is to be noted also that ON *þoll-r* 'beam' was first attested in Normandy as *tollet*, now *tolet* 'thole-pin'.

[r], [-rr] and [ʀ]

ODan. [r] was regularly treated as Romance [r]: ON *dreng-r* 'rope' > ONorm. *drenc* 'rope, truss'; ON *rás* 'course, channel' > Fr. *ras* 'current'; ON *Hrólf-r, Rólf-r* + *villa* > ONorm. *Rol villa* > *Rouville* (J. A. des Gautries, p. 399). There are no reliable examples of ODan. [-rr] in France other than ODan. **knarr* (cf. OIcel. *knǫrr*, gen. *knarrar*) 'ship' which is attested as OF *kenart, canart* 'type of ship'. The flexional ending *-r* in ON words does not, of course, appear in OF words, with one important exception: Norm. *har* < ON *há-r* 'dog-fish' (v. Glossary §90).[40] At a later period there was frequent assimilation of [r] to a following [l]: ON *kerling*, ODan. **karling* > ONorm. *calingue;* Fr. *carlingue* 'keelson'. This change was of course common not only in words of ON origin; the final element of *Saint-Martin-de-la-Bellouse* appeared as *Berlosa* in the 11th century.[41] Cf. also the form *pelles* for *perles* in the *Roman de la Rose*, and *palle* for *parle* in Guiart's *Branche des royaux lignages*.[42]

There are no reliable examples in Normandy of words with ON [ʀ], which was probably a sound intermediate between [z] and [r], from Primitive Gmc. [z].

[m] and [-mm]

ODan. [m] and [-mm] were both identified with Romance [m], there being probably no distinction between the simple and the lengthened consonant in Neustria in 900. There are, however, few reliable examples of ODan. [-mm] in Normandy; names such as ODan. *Tummi* and *Skammel(s)* also occurred without the geminate. In Normandy these names occur in *Tummavilla* attested in 1080 and *Scamelli-villa,* now *Equemauville* (J. A. des Gautries, 412-3, 422). Examples of ODan. [m] in Normandy are: ON *humar-r* 'lobster'> ONorm. *houmar,* Fr. *homard* 'lobster'; ON *mar-r* 'sea'> ONorm., Fr. *mare* 'pool, pond'.

When final after a vowel, [m] was replaced by [n] by the Romance speakers. E. Richter gives the date of the change of final [m] to [n] as the 8th century;[43] the form *oram* in *Eulalie* is not necessarily an indication that [m] was pronounced in final position in 880.[44] There was replacement of [m] by [n] in: ODan. *Tummi, Tommi* + *villa*> ONorm. *Thomevilla* in 1238> *Tonneville,* and also ODan. *Skam(m)el(s)* + *topt*> *Scameltot* 1087-90> now *Cannetot,* also *Ecannetot* (J. A. des Gautries, pp. 413, 422). In Norm. *Hougerville* (< ODan. *Holmgeirr* + *villa*) [m] was effaced in the consonant cluster.

[n] and [nn]

ODan. [n] and [nn] were treated as Romance [n]: ODan. *flundra*> Norm. flondre; ON *flana* 'to run about'> Fr. *flâner.* A special development took place in ON *stafn* 'stem' in the change to ONorm. °*estavne*> °*estavre*> *étrave.* ONorm. °*estavne* also gave °*estavle* which became *étable* and *étauve.*[45] Similarly ODan. °*hafn* (cf. OIcel. *hǫfn*) is probably the source of ONorm. *havene* and *hable,* LL *haula* and Fr. *havre.* Cf. OF *juevre*< *juevne*< Lat. *junior* contaminated with °*juvenior* (Pope, p. 230). Final [-n] after a consonant was lost very early: ON *Biǫrn*> ONorm. *Bier.* When [n] was in the middle of an ON consonant cluster, the Romance speakers simplified the cluster by dropping [n]: ON *Arnfast-r* > ONorm. *Arfast*; ON *Arnketill* > ONorm. *Architellus*.[46] When ON [-n] was preceded by [v], the Romance speakers added [ə], since [-vn] did not exist in Romance: ON *stafn* > ONorm. **estavne* > Fr. *étrave* 'stem'; ODan. **hafn* 'harbor' > ONorm. *havene* > Fr. *havre*. The Romance treatment of ON *hún-n* 'knob at the top of the mast-head' and ON *grunn-r* 'bottom (of sea)' is unusual in that the words received a final vowel in Romance: *hune* 'top', *grune* 'bas-fond'.[47] ON *dún-n* 'down' appeared in the 12th century as *dum*, and also as OF *dumet, donnet*, Norm. *dun, dumet, deumet* and the unusual form *duvet*, which might be a Breton development of the word.[48] After nasalization of the preceding vowel took place before a former nasal consonant, there was hesitation between the use of [m] and [n] when a suffix was added, as in Norm. *godoner* 'to swear' from Eng. *God damn*.[49] Thus ON *hamp-r* 'hemp' > Norm. *han, hanette*; ON *dún-n* > OF *dum, dumet, donnet*; ON *rúm* > ONorm. *run*, OF *arumer*, Norm. *arruner*.

[w]

It is quite probable that the Romance speakers of Neustria had the phoneme [w-] in initial position before 900 since there had been considerable Germanic influence in that region. ON words with initial [w-] were pronounced with [w-] by the Romance speakers: ON *virki* 'fortress' > *Wirchia*; ON *veif* 'something flapping or waving' > LL *waiva*, AN *waif*;[50] ON *vinda* 'to hoist' > ONorm. *windé*, p. p. of unattested ONorm. **winder*. Some time after the 11th century, a shift of initial [w-] to [v-] must have begun along the coastal areas of Normandy.[51] At this time Central French was using [gw-] word initial (< Germanic [w-]); between the [v] area and the [gw] area there was a slowly diminishing area where [w-] was still pronounced. Thus initial [v], [w], and [gw-] must have been variants of the same phoneme, and Norm. words with initial [w-] which reached Paris in the early period were automatically pronounced with [gw-].[52] Examples of the word-for-word change from initial [w-] to [v-] or [gw-] in Norman place-names not of ON origin are: *Vibray*

(1066), now *Guibray* (Falaise, C.); *Watredi villa,* now *Varre-ville,* M.; *Wasuic, Guasvic, Guasuit,* 11th c., now *Vasouy* (Hon-fleur, C.); *Wavreti,* now *Gavrai,* M.[53] Cf. also the Germanic name *Vautier* in northern Normandy and *Gautier* in southern Normandy.[54] Thus ON *vindáss* 'windlass' is attested as ONorm. *windas,* Fr. *guindas* (from earlier °[gwindas]) and Fr. *vindas,* a word from Normandy after the change from [w] to [v] took place; cf. also ON *veðr-viti* 'weather-vane'> ONorm. *wirewite*> Fr. *girouette,* Jersey *virouette* 'weather-vane'.

For ON [w] in position other than initial, cf. ON *þveit* 'clearing of land'> Norm. *-t(h)uit* in place-names; ON *Sveinn* attested in Normandy as *Svenus,* 11th c. with *v* representing a semi-consonant (J. A. des Gautries, p. 318). If Fr. *gouine* is from ON *kvinna* 'woman' (cf. Littré, s.v. *gouine*), there must have been some Breton influence in the development of [gw-] from [kw-], since such a change is hardly to be expected in Normandy. In the early contact between the Vikings of Nor-mandy and the Bretons, it is possible that some Norman words of ON origin became part of the Breton language.[55]

[j]

In the 7th century, initial [j] in Gallo-Roman had closed to [ǧ] with the result that initial [j] did not exist in the sound system of north-western French in 900.[56] When ON words with initial [j] were taken into the Romance dialect of Neustria, they may have been pronounced with [ǧ] by the Romance speakers; however there are few examples to prove that this was the case. Perhaps ON *jol* 'Yule'> Fr. *joli*; ON °*jarð-not*> Norm. *gernotte* 'earth-nut'.[57] The strengthening of [j] to [ǧ] is analogous to that of [w-] to [gw-]. Cf. also AN *daie* 'servant' which may be from ON *deigja* 'maid' and not from ME *daye* which is probably also of ON origin.[58]

The Romance Treatment of the Old Danish Vowels and Diphthongs.

[ā] and [ă] in Stressed Syllables.

Since Old French did not distinguish phonemically between [ā] and [ă] in the 9th and 10th centuries, the two vowels will be treated together. They were both treated as OF [a], the quality of the vowel depending on its position in the OF word and the nature of the surrounding consonants: ON *flana*> Fr. *flâner* 'to lounge about'; ON *gabba* 'to mock'> OF *gaber* 'to mock'; ON *vindáss*> Fr. *guindas, vindas* 'windlass'. In parts of Normandy, [a] followed by [n] developed to [āo], as in Norm. [flawne] (Fr. *flâner*).[59] Before [r] we have to reckon with the alternation of [ar] and [er] as in Fr. *asperge* for older *asparge*, Fr. *épervier* (< Gmc. *sparwari*); thus ODan. *Starr* + *villa* is attested as *Starvilla, Estarvilla*, but today is *Eterville*.[60] [a] + [l] + consonant developed to [al]> [au]> [o] long after the Viking period, although the change started in the 9th century (Pope, p. 158). Thus ODan. *Malti* + *villa*> *Maltevilla* in 1059> *Motteville*, S.-I. (J. A. des Gautries, p. 409); cf. ON *hjalm* 'rudder' > OF *jaume*, Fr. *jaumière* 'rudder hole'.

The sound represented in Old Icelandic spelling by ǫ resulted from the process known as u-mutation of [a]. This process had not taken place in Denmark at the time of the settlement of Normandy and the Danelaw, judging by linguistic evidence. ME *haggen* 'to cut' and *dag* 'dew' did not come from OIcel. *hǫggva* and *dǫgg*, but frcm ODan. forms with [a]. Thus the fact that OIcel. words have ǫ is no indication that certain Fr. words with [a] are not of ON origin. Marstrander, p. 74 and Björkman, p. 288 found that the Irish and English regularly used *a* in ON words when the OIcel. form had ǫ. Thus OF *havene*, Fr. *havre* 'port' must be from an unmutated ODan. *hafn, rather than from OIcel. *hǫfn*. OF *lagan* 'debris d'un vaisseau que la mer jette sur le rivage' may come from ODan. *lagn (cf. OIcel. *lǫgn*, pl. *lagnir* 'net laid in the sea', 'goods or wreckage lying on the bed of the sea'). ONorm. *lage* 'law' is probably from ODan. *lag (cf. OIcel. *lǫg* 'law' and Eng. *law* of ON origin).

[ă] in Unstressed Syllables.

It has been stated that the change of French final and intertonic [a] to [ə] took place during the 8th and 9th centuries.[61] Only [ə] remained as a vowel in unstressed syllables, and consequently all ON unstressed vowels were to be rendered as [ə]. Cf. ON *snekkja* > ONorm. *°snekkə* > ONorm. *esneque* 'type of ship'; ON *hora* 'whore' > Norm. *hore* 'girl'. Cf. also the ODan. name *Tōfa* appearing in the place-name *Le Mesnil-Tôve* (J. A. des Gautries, pp. 146-7).

[ē]

Björkman found [ē] to be a rare sound in the older Scandinavian languages and rarer still in the Viking period than in the later literary period.[62] The sound was rare in ON words in English, and in Normandy the sound appears to be rare in the ON words which became part of the dialect of that region. ODan. *bētas* (cf. OIcel. *beiti-áss*) 'sail-yard' > ONorm. *betas* 'sail-yard'; ODan. *Hēlgi* + *villa* > *Helgevilla* > *Heuqueville, Heugueville*. On the other hand *Herquetot, Herqueville* and *Herquemoulin* are probably from an ONorw. *Helgi* with short [ĕ] (J. A. des Gautries, p. 108) with the development: *Helgevilla* > *Herqueville*, etc.

[ĕ]

In addition to ONorw. *Helgi* + *villa*, which gave *Helgevilla, Herqueville*, there are many other examples of ODan. [ĕ] in Normandy: ON *bekk-r* > Norm. *bec* 'brook' in place-names; ON *dreng-r* 'cable' > ONorm. *drenc* 'rope'. In a few cases French has [i] where ON had [e]: ON *telgja* 'to cut' > Fr. *tille* 'cooper's adze' and ON *kveld-ulf-r* > OF *guildrou*, Fr. *guilledou;* there may have been influence of the palatal to account for the change of [e] to [i]; cf. Lat. *tilium* > *°tel'u* > OF *til* (Pope, p. 165). In most of the forms attested before 1035, the Norman forms have *e*, as do the ON forms, in *Anschetil, Torchetil* (from ON *Ásketill, þorketill,* resp.), but the later forms have *i*: *Anschitil, Turchitil* (J. A. des Cautries, p. 245, n. 11). This may be assimilation to the following [i]. This theory is corroborated by the fact that in many of the early place-names with these elements, *e* occurs in the two syllables: *Anschetevilla, Ansketelvilla, Ansquetevilla, Torquetevilla, Turchetevilla* (J. A. des Gautries, pp. 383, 429).

[ī] and [ĭ] in Stressed Syllables.

ON [ī] and [ĭ] were regularly treated as Romance [i]: ON °*vígi-bord*> Fr. *vibord* 'sheer-strake'; ON *flikki* 'flitch'> Norm. *flique* 'flitch of bacon'; ON *skipari* 'sailor'> ONorm. *eskipre* 'pilot'. ON *virki* 'fortress' appeared as *Wircia, Guircia, Gercia, La Guirce, Guiercia,* with the modern forms *La Guerche* and *La Guierche*.[63] The influence of the following [r] was important in this word. ON *sild* 'herring' appears in France only with *e*: *selletan, célerin, célan;* followed by two consonants, ON [i] probably sounded more like [e] to the Romance speakers than it did like OF [i]. Cf. also Glossary §116 for the change, *fliche*> *flèche,* 'flitch of bacon'.

[ĭ] in Unstressed Syllables.

Before the time of the Viking settlement of Neustria, final [i] in French had developed to [ə]; this accounts for the Romance treatment of ODan. unstressed [ĭ] as Romance [ə]. ON *Ketil-l* is attested as ONorm. *Chetellus* and also in such compounds as *Chetelvilla* (J. A. des Gautries, p. 119). Cf. also ON *biti*> Fr. *bitte* 'bollard'; ON *kriki* 'bay'> Norm. *crique* 'bay'. An unusual form is *Tovi* (from ODan. *Tōfi*) but the form is a genitive (J. A. des Gautries, p. 318) and perhaps has a Latin ending, as does the form *Thovo* from the same ON name.

[ō] and [ŏ]

ODan. [ō] and [ŏ] were usually treated as OF [o], the quality of the OF vowel depending on the position in the word: ON *flóna* 'to become warm'> Norm. *floner* 'to become angry'; ON *hóra* 'whore'> Norm. *hore* 'girl'; ON *kot* 'hut'> Norm. *-cot(t)e* (in place-names); ON *skora* 'to tally'> Norm. *écorer* 'to keep tally of fish'. In Norm. words there is occasionally an

alternation between [o] and [u]; thus ON *þorp* 'farm, etc.'>
Norm. *torp, tourp;* ON *trog* 'trough'> ONorm. *trou,* Norm. *tro*
'trough'. In countertonic syllables in French, [o] tends to become [u]: ON *toga* 'to tow'> Fr. *touer* 'to tow'; ON *bóglina*>
Fr. *bouline* 'bowline'. This is also true in Norm. place-names
derived from ON names beginning in *þor*-and *þór-* :*Tourville,*
Touffreville, Tourlaville, Tourmauville, etc. (J. A. des Gautries,
421-433). In the earliest attested forms of these names, both *o*
and *u* are found: *Torfvilla, Turvilla*< ON *Torf* + *villa; Turgis-*
torp, Torgisval, both from ON *þorgisl.* There is even a development to [y] in ON *þorgaut-r* + *villa*> *Torgovilla,* 1215> *Tur-*
gauville, and also ON *þorir* or ODan. *þóri*> *Toretot,* 1222>
Turretot. It would seem that the development of ODan. [ō]
and [ŏ] in Normandy was dependent on conditions in the
phonology of the Romance dialect spoken there rather than
on the length of the Danish vowel in question.[64]

Norm. place-names in *-beuf* and *-fleur* cannot be derived
from ON *bu* (ODan. *both*) and ON *flo* since the earlier forms
in *-buet* and *-flet* show the results of diphthongization of older
Germanic loans, a process which had ceased long before 900.[65]

[ū]

ODan. [ū] was treated by the Romance speakers as [ū],
which in 900 was probably in the course of change to [y][66]:
ON *Múli* + *topt*> Norm. *Le Multot;* ON *Rúni* + *topt*> *Rune-*
tot; ON *Skúli* + *topt*> *Ecultot;* ON *hún-n*> Fr. *hune* 'top'; ON
stein-n 'stone' + *hús* 'house'> *Etainhus.* A later Norman development of [y] to [œ] took place in some areas: Norm., Fr. *hune*
'top of mast'> Thaon *heune* 'head'; Norm. *bruman* (< ON
*bruð-mann) 'bridegroom'> Thaon *brœmā.*

[ŭ]

ODan. words with [ŭ] appear in the oldest Norman documents with *u,* and less often with *o.* The modern forms regularly
have [o] in the words in question: ON *Gunnulf-r*> *Gunnovilla*
ca. 1067-1200; ON *Ámundi*> *Amundi villa,* 990> *Mondeville;*[67]
ON *Ásulf-r* or *Ōsulf-r*> *Osulvila* ca. 1015> *Auzouville;*[68] ON

Azurr > *Adsor, Azor,* 11th century; ODan. *Gunni* > *Gonnevilla,* ca. 1024 *Gonneville* (J. A. des Gautries, pp. 303-4, 393). At the time when OF [ū] was developing to [y], the ON words with short [ŭ] appear with *u;* it would be difficult to prove that Old French still had short [ŭ] at that time, but it would seem likely on the basis of the orthography. If that is not the case, then *u* must have represented the sound [ǫ] in the early documents. Other examples taken from vocabulary are: ODan. *flundra* > Norm. *flondre* 'flounder'; ON *tundr* 'tinder' > Norm. *tondre* 'tinder'; ON *humar-r* > Fr. *homard* 'lobster'.

[ǣ]

There are few reliable examples of this sound in Norman words of ON origin. Perhaps ON *bræða* 'to tar' > Fr. *brayer* 'to tar'. The etymology in the *FEW*, III, 4-5 for Fr. *dalle* (from ON *dæla* 'ship's pump') is phonetically difficult to justify as is the development of ON *snæfr* 'narrow, tough' to OF *esmièvre,* ONorm. *nièvre,* Fr. *mièvre* given in Bloch, s.v. *mièvre.*

[ø]

ODan. [ø] was equated with OF [e] in the name *þorfrøðr,* attested in Normandy as *Turfredus* and also in the place-names *Turfretvilla,* ca. 1040; *Torfrescalis,* 1156-1161; *Torfrevilla,* 1151; *Turfredivilla,* 1068, etc. There are also several examples of *ei:* *Turfreivilla, Mesnil Torfrei* from the 12th and 13th centuries, and one example of *Turfridi villa* (J. A. des Gautries, 319-320, 424-6). Björkman found no reliable case of ON short [ø] in Middle English and only a few examples of ON long [ø], which was treated as ME [ē].[69]

[ȳ] from earlier [iū], and [ỹ] from earlier [ŭ]

The ON personal name *Styrr* appeared in Normandy as *Esturus* and in the place-names *Sturivilla* and *Sturvilla,* today *Etreville* and *Eturville.* Similarly ON *Styrkárr* appears in the Norman names *Sturgarvilla, Sturcavilla, Turcaville.*[70] In the development of ON *bý-r* 'farm' to *-bye* in *Hambye,* it must have

EDINBURGH UNIVERSITY LIBRARY

CANCELLED

been the older stage [iu], rather than [ȳ] which was the sound in the word in 900. (Cf. below under the treatment of [io] and [iu]).[71]

[au]

The diphthong [au] was probably at the stage [ǫu] in Denmark in Viking times (cf. Skautrup, p. 125). Whatever the quality of the ODan. phoneme at this time, it seems to have been treated as OF [o], with a probable later development to [u] in parts of Normandy. Thus ON *Geirlaug* appears in Normandy as *Gerloc* and *þorgaut-r* appears as *Turgot* (J. A. des Gautries, p. 247). ON *haug-r* 'mound'> Norm. *hogue, hougue* 'hill'; ON *skaut* 'sheet of a sail'> ONorm. *escote*> Fr. *écoute* 'sheet of a sail'.

[øy]

There are few reliable identifiable reflexes of ON [øy] in Normandy. ONorm. *aye* 'small island' and the ending *-ey* in *Jersey* and *Guernsey* may be from ON *ey* 'island' or an ODan. **øy*.[72] ON *sneyða* 'to bereave' may have given ONorm. *esneier* 'to rid of'; OF *tristre* and *titre* 'poste de chasse' have been traced to ON *treysta*, ODan. *trøysta* 'to make safe, trust, dare'.[73] ON *Øysteinn* appears in the name *Usteinvilla*, ca. 1170, now *Inthéville*, M. (J. A. des Gautries, p. 433). The same ON name appears in Ireland as *Ostin, Oistin* and in the place-name *Baile Hostin* (Marstrander, p. 72). Luick, I[1], 389 states that [øy] was usually equated with ME [ei], as in ME *keiren* 'to go' (cf. OIcel. *keyra* 'to ride, drive').

[ia]

ON *tjald* 'tent for ships while not in use'> ONorm. *tialz* 'tente dressé sur un navire au repos'. There are, however, few reliable reflexes of ON [ia] in Normandy. The ON surname *Skialdari* is given by J. A. des Gautries as the source of Norm. *Sceldrevilla*, now *Equeurdreville*, but the 11th century form *Sceldreville*, like the English place-name *Skeldergate*, the name of a street in York, and Irish *scelu* (derived by Marstrander, pp. 77-79 from ON *skiald*) all seem to come from an ON form with [e]; i.e. the breaking of [e] to [ia] had not yet taken place when the words were introduced in Normandy and the British Isles. Skautrup sees in this an indication that no significant migration to England from Denmark must have taken place after ca. 900, the date usually accepted for the completion of breaking (v. Skautrup, I, 98). The term 'breaking' may be defined as incomplete mutation, caused chiefly by [a] and less often by [u].

[io] and [iu]

The ODan. diphthongs [io] and [iu] were probably stressed on the first element ca. 900;[74] since Old French did not have these diphthongs, they were treated as OF [ie], which was also stressed on the first element at that time. Thus Norm. *tierre* 'tether' must be from an ODan. *tiōðr* (cf. OIcel. *tjóðr*) 'tether'; the place-names *Dieppe* and *Dieppedalle* must be from ODan. *diūp* (cf. OIcel. *djúp*) 'deep water, deep place'; the ON name *Biǫrn* appears in Guillaume de Jumièges and Robert Wace as *Bier*. The ODan. form of OIcel. *stýri* 'rudder' must have been *stiūri* in 900 (cf. the form *stiuir* in Ireland and also *stiurusmand* which was from a form with [iu] rather than directly from OIcel. *stýri-maðr*; v. also n. 71). Thus ONorm. *estiere* 'rudder' must be from ODan. *stiūri*. Sjögren pp. 396 ff. derives Norm. *mielle* 'sand-bank' from an ON pl. *mjelar* related to OIcel. *mel-r* 'sand-bank' and also appearing in England as *miol* in place-names.

[ei]

The diphthong [ei] has been used by some scholars as a criterion to distinguish between Danish and Norwegian influence in Normandy. J. Jakobsen, *Danske Studier* (1911), 59-84 and A. Pedersen, *Danske Studier* (1911), 85-98 concluded that Danish influence must have been stronger than Norwegian; this theory was based partly on the fact that many Norman forms seemed to be derived from a monophthong [ē] rather than on the characteristic ONorw. [ei], Danish having simplified the diphthong.[75] However, if [ei] was still developing to [ē] ca. 900, which may certainly be the case, [ei] would not necessarily have to indicate Norwegian influence. The stronger Danish influence can be seen in a clearer manner in the Norman use of [v-] in such words as *varangue* and *varech*; Old Norwegian, having lost [w] before [r], would not have given these Norman forms. Similarly the absence of [h] before [r] and [n] in such names as *Rouville, Rol villa* in 1063 from ODan. *Rolf-r* rather than ONorw. *Hrolf-r*, and *Nacqueville* which must be from an ODan. *°Nakki* rather than from ONorw. *Hnakki* as well as the fact that ODan. names are well represented in Normandy whereas ONorw. names are rare, are more important and reliable criteria of Danish influence.

As for the Romance treatment of [ei], ONorw. *þveit* was adopted by the Romance speakers of Normandy at the time when Fr. *nuit* was at the stage *nueit,* with [uei] from an older [uoi].[76] Thus the Norman reflex of ONorw. *þveit* is *-t(h)uit,* a form appearing in the lower Seine valley and probably indicative of strong Norwegian influence there.[77] ON *Stein-n* or *stein-n* 'stone' appears in the forms *Esteintot, Staintot, Steintot,* attested in 1074 and 1198 (cf. the modern forms *Etheintot, Etaintot,* S.-I.) ON *þorstein-n* appears most commonly as *Torsten* and *Turstinus* in Normandy, with an example of *Tostein* and also the place-name *Tusteinmaisnil* attested in 1156. Similarity has been pointed out between the form *Turstinus* and the form *-stin* common in Danish and Swedish runic inscriptions as the result of reduction of [ei].[78] The name *Svein-n,* common in Denmark but rare in Norway in the early 10th century, appears as *Svenus* in Normandy, but ON *Óbeini* (*Úbeini*) appears in the form *Unbeina.*[79] ON *skeið* 'ship' and ON *greiði* 'arrangement' were treated as words with OF [ei], which later passed to [oi]; thus ON *skeið*> ONorm. *eskei*> OF *eschoi* 'ship', and ON *greiði*> OF *agrei*> *agroi* 'tackle, gear'. Cf. also the name of the converted Dane *Ansleicus* living in France ca. 864; ON *Ásleik-r* is later attested as *Anslec(h), Ansleccus* in the 10th and 11th centuries. This might reflect the change of ODan. [ei] to [e] in progress at the time. (v. J. A. des Gautries, p. 85).

[ã]

In the 10th century, Old Danish had nasal vowels as well as oral vowels, but in the Danish runic inscriptions only [ã] had a special symbol.[80] This is important because [ã] may have been the only ODan. nasal vowel to be identifiable in Normandy. The ONorm. name *Unbeina* (< ON *Ôbeini, Úbeini*) has [un] due to English influence, and the name itself is Anglo-Scandinavian (J. A. des Gautries, p. 126). Several ON names in [ãs-] appear in Normandy with *ans-*; this may be an indication that the Romance dialect spoken in Neustria already had a nasal vowel [ã] in 900. Thus ON *Ásketil-l* appears in Normandy as *Anschetillus, Anschitillus, Anschetil* and in place-names as *Anschetilvilla*, etc., today *Ancourteville, Ancretiéville*, etc. Similarly ON *Ásleik-r* appears as *Anslech, Anslechus* and in *Anslecvilla*, today *Anneville*. It seems unnecessary to attribute the *n* to Frankish influence, as Dauzat does in *Les Noms de famille de France*, p. 69.[81] Unfortunately the fact that ONorm. *Ansfred, Ansger* and *Ansgot* may be West Germanic as well as Norse makes it impossible to be absolutely certain about the fate of ODan. [ã] in Normandy. In words other than the personal names in *Ás-*, there is no evidence of the ODan. nasal vowel being represented in Romance pronunciation or orthography.[82]

Morphology

There is little evidence of morphological influence of Old Danish in the words and names which appeared in Normandy. The name *Mulambec* (< ON *Múlabekk-r*) seems to contain the ON genitive (J. A. des Gautries, p. 125, n. 71). It has been suggested that Fr. *quille* 'keel' is derived from a plural or dative singular form (*FEW*, II, 726,). There is a similarity in the construction of the phrase *a flote* in Old French and the ON prepositional phrase *á floti* 'afloat'. A most unusual case is that of Norm. *har* 'dogfish' taken into Romance with the ON nominative singular ending -*r*; cf. ON *há-r* 'dogfish'.

Contaminations

A number of French words of Norse origin have undergone changes other than phonetic. In some Norse words, the final member ceased to be a meaningful element after becoming part of standard French, and was sometimes replaced by a French suffix. Thus, *guindas* > *guindeau*; *havenet* > *haveneau*; *°herr-nest* > *hernais* > *harnais*; *dranet* (< ON *drag-net*) seems to have been associated with French words in -*et* and in -*ette*, hence the forms *dranet* and *drainette*, the latter also having been influenced by *drainer*. Fr. *girouette* probably would have been *°guirouette* were it not for the existence of the verb *girer*, and ONorm. *wirewite* with the same meaning would have been *°werewite* but for the association with the verb *virer*, according to A. Thomas, *Essais de philologie française*, p. 401.

An ONorm. *°bacbord* may have been influenced by the adjective *bas* to give OF *basbord* > *bâbord*. Norman *bruman* in the meaning of 'son-in-law' seems to have been associated with *bru* 'daughter-in-law,' but the original meaning of 'bridegroom' also survives. OF *sigler*, according to several etymological dictionaries, has been crossed with *cingler* 'to strike' to give the modern *cingler* 'to sail'. If Norman *havron* 'oats' is from ON *hafri* 'oats' (cf. English dialect *haver* also from Norse) there may have been crossing with *avenon* 'oats' (< Latin *avena*). Fr. *colin, cole* in the fourteenth century may have been from the ON form of Swedish *kolja*; Dutch and English words for this fish do not exist without the element -*fish*: English *coalfish*, Dutch *koolvis(ch)*; crossing with the proper name *Colin* is likely. The Norman *héri* 'male hare' may owe its suffix to OF *connil*; Norman *loure* 'musette, etc.' may owe its vowel to influence of Latin *lura*; Fr. *flèche* < OF *fliche*, Norman *flique* may have been contaminated by *flec* of Picard origin coming in from the Low Countries. The nautical term *bonnette* *en étui* from an older *estoinc* and *estouin* 'studding-sail' seems to have been associated with Fr. *étui* 'box, etc.'. *Homard* has been classed with words in *-ard*; for the complex history of the words *flot* and *flotte* with mention of possible contaminations, cf. the *FEW*, III, 626b–627a and 640. The similarity between Le Havre *higuère* 'yesterday' and ON *i gær* with identical meaning may be a coincidence; Old Gascon and Bearnais have forms with [g] also which may be an unusual phonetic development of Latin *heri* > [ier] > [iwer] > [igwer] > [iger].

PART II

LEXICON OF FRENCH AND NORMAN WORDS

OF SCANDINAVIAN ORIGIN

LEXICON OF FRENCH AND NORMAN WORDS
OF SCANDINAVIAN ORIGIN

Introduction

The lexicon of French and Norman words of Scandinavian origin that follows has been arranged according to various semantic spheres, with the exception of recent borrowings, which have been grouped together in the final sections. For determining which words are of Scandinavian origin, the following criteria have been used: first, the fact that the word in question is known to have existed in the older Scandinavian languages; second, the fact that the word was first attested in Normandy, or is still in use only there and in neighboring provinces; third, the phonetic factors based on the phonology of Old Danish and of the Romance dialect of Neustria in the early tenth century; fourth, the fact that a given Norse word was integrated not only in the Romance of Neustria but also in other areas where Scandinavians settled, such as England and Russia; and fifth, the fact that the Vikings were particularly advanced in matters relating to navigation and fishing, a factor which left its mark on the Norman vocabulary.

It can be seen from the *FEW* that a large number of Norse words exist not only in Normandy, but also in the nearby provinces of the West: Maine, Anjou and Poitou; this lexicon does not include all Norse words that have spread from Normandy to neighboring areas, nor have we sought to solve the problem of whether the Vikings left any direct influence on the vocabulary of the patois of the western provinces, or whether it was the bilingual Romanized Normans of the following generations who were responsible for introducing certain words into the provinces south of Normandy. The fact that a given word has never been attested in any of the

older Scandinavian languages may in some cases be accidental; however, we have thought it preferable to omit such
words. Among these are *haler*, attested since the twelfth century in Norman texts, and which the *DG*, Gamillscheg 503b,
REW 3997, Kluge, s.v. *holen*, and Guerlin de Guer, *Le Parler populaire de la commune de Thaon*, s.v. *haler*, all derive from Old
Norse; however, according to Hellquist, s.v. *hala*, and Falk-
Torp, s.v. *hale*, the modern Scandinavian words are of Dutch
origin. Similarly Fr. *lof* 'côté du navire frappé par le vent'
is in the opinion of Dauzat, the *REW* 5102, Alessio, I, 294, and
the *DG* from ON *lóf*, but again, according to Hellquist, s.v.
lov, 3, and Falk-Torp, s.v. *luv*, the Swedish and Danish words
are not native Scandinavian words. The same can be said of
Fr. *hisser*, which the *DG* and the *REW* 4119 derive from
Swedish *hissa*; and Fr. *turbot*, which Bloch, Dauzat, the *REW*
8795, Frahm, p. 24 and W. von Wartburg, *Évolution et structure de la langue française*, pp. 72-73 all trace to ON *þorn-butr*,
in spite of the fact that not only did this compound not exist in
Old Norse, but the second element is itself a Low German
loan-word in Swedish, according to Hellquist, s.v. *butta*. The
FEW, I, 364a, derives Norman *blet* 'image' (patois of Avranches
and La Hague) from ON *bilæti* 'picture', but this word is only
attested in later Old Norse where it seems to be a West Germanic borrowing (cf. Kluge, s.v. *Bild*).

No attempt has been made to discuss every Norse etymology
ever presented for French words; a number of these were
too fantastic semantically and phonetically to merit serious
consideration.

Naval Architecture and Navigation

1. *agréer*, v. tr. 'équiper', in use 12th–19th c., first attested in forms *agreier*, *agroier*; formed from *gréer* 'to rig'
(< ON *greiða*, v. tr. 'to unravel, arrange'), but *gréer* was not
widely used until 1716 when used by Frézier in *Relation du
voyage de la mer du Sud*; *gréer* was admitted by the Academy
in 1798 (*DG*), but is much older than the 18th c.; cf. Guern-

sey *grâie* 'revêtir, nettoyer' (Gamillscheg 18b), Aldèrney, Sark, Guernsey *grà* 'vêtir' (*ALF* Map 1381). Derived forms: *grée-ment*, s.m. 'rigging, gear', 1670; *dégréer, désagréer,* v. tr. 'to unrig', 1672, 1688; *dégré(e)ment,* s.m. 'unrigging, dismantling, stripping of mast', 1873; *dégréage,* s.m. 'unrigging'; *gréage,* s.m. 'rigging gear'; *gréeur,* s.m. 'rigger', Acad. 1835; *ragréer,* v. tr. 'to re-rig', 1554, admitted by Acad. as *raggreer,* 1718; cf. *ra-gréer sa réputation* 'to restore one's reputation'; *ragré(e)ment,* s.m. 're-rigging, cleaning down of brick-work', Acad. 1762; Al-derney *agræ,* v. tr. 'atteler'; Sark *agré,* v. tr. 'atteler' (*ALF,* Map 66). Cf. Bloch, s.v. *agrès; DG;* Valkhoff, s.v. *agréer;* Tob-ler, s.v. *agroier.*

2. *agrès,* s.m. pl. 'tackle, gear', 12th c. (Tobler, s.v. *agroi*) in *Roman de Rou* in the form *agrei.* Frahm, p. 59 mentions OF *gree* as the source; from ON *greiði,* s.m. 'disentanglement, arrangement' (*REW* 3859a) attested in 1491 with specific ref-erence to ships in the form *aggrais* (Bloch). Cf. Dauzat, s.v. *agréer* and Falk, p. 70, n. 1; a Dutch origin is given by Littré, *DG,* Larousse, Saggau 62, Valkhoff, s.v. *agrei.*

3. *arrimer,* v. tr. 'to stow away', 1398 (Bloch), probably related to ON *rýma* 'to make more roomy, clear, prepare the way for' rather than ME *rimen.* In the 15th and 16th c. *arrimer* meant 'arranger, disposer (en général)', a meaning close to the ON word. Cf. also OF *arumer, arruner* of ON origin, below §49, and the form *arrinné* in a text from 1532 (Huguet, s.v. *arruner*). *arrimage,* s.m. 'stowing', 1398; *arrimeur,* s.m. 'stower', 1398; *désarrimage,* s.m. 'shifting of cargo'; *désarrimer* v. tr. 'to unstow, put ship out of trim'; *se désarrimer,* v.r. 'to shift' (of cargo); *réarrimage,* s.m. 'restowing'; *réarrimer,* v. tr. 'to restow'.

4. *bâbord,* s.m. 'larboard', attested in 1529 as *basbord,* associated with Fr. *bas* through popular etymology, probably from ON *bak-borði* 'larboard' (Dauzat, *Histoire de la langue française,* p. 187; Frahm, p. 58; *DG,* p. 18; Sainéan, *La Langue de Rabelais,* I, 107). A Dutch etymology is found in the *REW,* 2nd ed., 872; *FEW,* II, 208a; Dauzat; *DG,* s.v. *bâbord;* Falk-Torp, s.v. *bagbord.* The appearance of the word in Italian in the 16th c. makes it evident that the Fr. word is much older than the 16th c. (Battisti-Alessio, s.v. *babordo*) as does the

existence of Sp. *babor* and Port. *bombordo*. Derived form: *bâbordais*, s.m. 'man of the port watch'.

5. *bardeau*, s.m. 'small raft of floating timber' may be from ON *barði* 'a sort of ship' (*FEW*, I, 253a, n. 7).

6. ONorm. *betas*, s.m. 'sail-yard'< ODan. *bētās (cf. OSwed. *bētās*, OIcel. *beiti-áss* 'sail-yard'). The ONorm. word is in Wace, *Roman de Brut*. Björkman, pp. 61, 98 states that ME *betas* may be from Norman rather than directly from Norse. ONorm. *betas* is discussed by Falk, p. 61 and Nyrop, *Wörter und Sachen*, VII (1921), 97. Godefroy I, 640c believed ONorm. *betas* to be of Sp. origin, while Tobler wonders whether *betas* is of English origin.

7. *bidon*, s.m. 'grog-tub, can, oil-drum, canteen, belly', first attested in the 15th c. in Norm. texts, may be of ON origin (cf. Icel. *biða, byða*, s.f. 'small wooden vessel'). The ON origin of *bidon* is given by Bloch, Dauzat, *FEW*, I, 354b, *REW* 1088. However, since ON [-ð-] was treated as OF [-ð-] and subsequently lost, the [-d-] of *bidon* is unusual. We might reckon with an expressive gemination of ON [ð] which would have resulted in [-dd-], which then would have yielded Fr. [-d-]. Cf. §111 and §207. A derived form is Parisian *bidonner* 'to drink' (*FEW*, I, 354b). If Norm. *bie*, s.f. 'cruche, toute sorte de vase' is the same word, it is the normal phonetic outcome of the ON form. However Dubois and Duméril derive Norm. *bie* from OF *buie*, s.f. 'cruche'.

8. *bitte*, s.f. 'bitt, bollard', first attested in a Rouen text in 1382 is from ON *biti*, s.m. 'cross-beam' (Bloch, Dauzat, *FEW*, I, 384b–385). Cf. Norm. *bitte* in use in the 16th c. in the meaning 'freestone' probably from the primary meaning of the ON word 'bit, small piece' (Sjögren, 385-6); cf. also Fr. *bitte* in the sense 'membrum virile'. The *FEW* gives the following derived forms: *biton, bitou*, s.m. 'pièce de bois sur laquelle s'attachent les amarres', in Rabelais (Huguet, s.v. *biton*); *bitton* 'petite bitte' also in Rabelais; *bittonières*, s.f. pl. 'égouts qui règnent à fond de cale de proue à poupe . . . pour conduire les eaux à la pompe'; *bitture*, s.f. 'range of cable, stiff glass of grog', 1683; *bitturer*, v. tr. 'to make drunk'; *se bitturer*, v.r. 'to get drunk'; *bitter*, v. tr. 'to bit (cable)', 1690; *débitter*,

v. tr. 'to unbit', 1687; *débiter*, v. tr. 'découper du bois de construction', 1387, also applied to other building materials, cloth, meat; hence Fr. *débiter* 'to cut up (stones, carcass, etc.)', 1870. Since 1464 *débiter* has also been used in the sense 'to sell at retail', a special semantic development from that of 'débiter du bois de construction', and from that meaning, the further development to 'détailler en récitant' came about, being first attested in the 17th c. in the meaning 'to recite'. Among the derivatives of *débiter* in its various meanings are: *débit*, s.m. 'retail sale', 1565; 'retail store', 1829; Norm. *être de débit* 'd'une vente facile'; Fr. *débitant*, s.m. 'retailer,' originally 'tobacconist', 1731; Thaon *k a bõ dbi* 'qui parle facilement'; Fr. *débiteur*, s.m. 'utterer', 1611 (Bloch); *débitable*, adj. 'that can be cut up'; *débitage*, s.m. 'cutting up'. Fr. *bitte* is also discussed by Saggau, p. 130; *REW* 1135; Falk, p. 47 and the *DG*, all of whom, together with Bloch, Dauzat and the *FEW*, agree on the ON origin of the word. It. *bitta* was attested in the 16th c. (Battisti-Alessio).

9. *bord*, s.m. 'board of ship' may be from ON *borð* 'board' (*DG*, p. 18). But the *DG*, s.v. *bord*, gives a Low German origin, whereas Bloch gives a Frankish source. The *FEW*, I, 436a, and the *REW* 1215 give the source simply as Germanic. OF *bort* 'pièce de bois courbe . . . réservée pour la marine' (Godefroy) may be from ON *borð*, s.n. 'board, plank' (*FEW*, I, 439b, n. 6) and may survive in Fr. *plat-bord*, s.m. 'gunwale'.

10. *bouline*, s.f. 'bowline', first attested in an Anglo-Norman work, *La Vie de Saint Gilles* in the 12th c. as *boesline*, is probably from ON *bóglina*, s.f. 'bowline' (Frahm, p. 66, *DG*, p. 18) rather than from English as stated by Bloch, Dauzat, *REW* 1248 and *FEW*, I, 477a, the latter work hesitating between Dutch and English as the source. However, Hellquist, s.v. *bolin* says that Eng. *bowline* is possibly from Norse; the *OED's* statement that ON *bóglina* is suspect does not seem justified, ON *bóglina* occurring in a list of synonyms at the end of the *Skaldskaparmál* in the *Prose Edda* (cf. *Edda Snorra Sturlusonar*, ed. Þorleifr Jónsson, p. 191, 1. 27). Cf. also the form *boline* in the *Roman de Tristan* (Tobler, s.v. *boeline*). Derived forms: *boulinage*, s.m. 'sailing close-hauled'; *bouliner*, v. tr. 'to haul (a sail) windward'; v.i. 'to sail close to the wind'; *boulinier*,

adj. 'weatherly'; s.m. 'ship that sails well to windward'. Cf. also *courir la bouline* 'to run the gauntlet'.

11.   *brayer,* v. tr. 'to pitch, tar', attested in the 13th c., seems to be from ON *bræða* 'to tar'. Fr. *brai* is attested in the 14th c. and Norm. *brē* is widely used (*ALF* 1054, *FEW*, I, 508b). Cf. also Jersey *bra* 'poix des cordonniers' (< ON *bráð* 'pitch'); cf. below §210. Cf. also Nyrop, *Wörter und Sachen,* VII (1921), 97; *REW* 1260 and Falk, p. 51. Bloch and Dauzat give a Gaulish source for the word.

12.   ONorm. *brant,* s.m. 'proue ayant la forme d'une lame d'épée' is from ON *brand-r* 'ship's beak'. ONorm. *brant* was used by Wace in the *Roman de Rou,* and is discussed by Sjögren, p. 399; *REW* 1274; *FEW*, I, 504a; Godefroy, I, 723a; Tobler, s.v. *brant*; Frahm, p. 54 and Falk, p. 44. Cf. ME *brand* also of ON origin (Sandahl, pp. 38 ff.).

13.   OF *bulcke* 'ce que la cale contient de marchandises' is either from Eng. *bulk* or ON *bulki* 'bulk' (*FEW*, I, 607b).

14.   OF *busse, buce, buse, bucze,* s.f. 'bateau très large' is related to ON *búza, buza,* s.f. 'sort of merchant ship', but ON *búza* is probably itself of Greek origin (Walther Vogel, "Nordische Seefahrten im früheren Mittelalter," *Meereskunde,* I (1907), 1-40). The ON word, first attested in Old Icelandic in 1251 (Cleasby-Vigfusson) was probably introduced to France through medieval commerce, but was attested as early as 1170 in French. Cf. Russian *busa* attested ca. 1200 also of probable ON origin (Falk, p. 110). Fr. *busse* is treated in the *FEW*, I, 667a; Kluge, *Seemannssprache,* p. 167; Dauzat; Valkhoff; Falk, p. 110; Kemna, p. 145; and Frahm, p. 47. Cf. also Godefroy, I, 762b and Tobler, s.v. *buce.*

14b.   OF *calingue,* Fr. *carlingue,* s.f. 'keelson'·ODan. °*karling,* given by Skautrup as the Danish form ca. 900 (cf. OIcel. *kerling,* s.f. 'old lady, one of the timbers supporting the planks of the deck'). OF *calingue,* attested in 1382, shows effects of assimilation of the [r] to the following [l], but the original form with [r] must have survived in Normandy, though unattested in the written language until 1600. The primary meaning 'old lady' in ON probably accounts for the feminine gender in French; otherwise [-ng] would have become voiceless as in OF *drenc, estrenc* 'rope'. Among the derived forms in the *FEW*, II, 605b are: Fr. *escarlingue*, 1678; *écarlingue* (*Encyclopédie*); Prov. *carlingo*, and Breton *garlink*. Since the advent of aviation, *carlingue* has become the Fr. word for 'cockpit'; cf. also *carlingage*, s.m. 'engine-bed'. The word *carlingue* is also discussed by Bloch, Dauzat and Falk, p. 56.

15. OPic. *canart*, AN *kenart* 'type of ship' may be from ON *knarri*, cf. OIcel. *knǫrr*, gen. *knarrar*, s.m. 'ship' (Frahm, p. 47; Falk, p. 109). The vowel is anaptyctic, and final *t* is non-etymological; cf. the form *kenar* in *La Vie de St. Gilles* (Tobler, s.v. *canart*). The *FEW*, II, 802a states that AN *kenart* was taken directly from ON rather than from AS *cnear*. Cf. also the example in Orderic Vital: "Quatuor naves magnae quas canardos vocant, de Norwegia in Angliam appulsae sunt" (Godefroy, I, 775).

16. *cingler*, v.i. 'to sail', OF *sigler* 'to sail' < ON *sigla* 'to sail'. OF *sigler* was first attested in the *Chanson de Roland*, ca. 1080 (Bloch, s.v. *cingler*) and by the end of the 14th century had become *singler* by contamination with *cingler* 'frapper avec une baguette flexible', the ship sailing (singlant) by means of the lashing wind (vent qui cingle) in the explanation given by Bloch. Cf. also OF *singlement*, s.m. 'battement des ailes'. A derivative of *sigler* was *sigleüre*, s.f. 'action de sigler; voyage sous voile'. From *cingler* the noun *cinglage*, s.m. 'sailing, ship's run' is derived. See also OF *sigle* below.

17. *dalle*, s.f. 'flagstone, paving-stone, floor tile' and *dalot*, s.m. in the expression *dalot de pont* 'scupper hole' and *dalot de pompe*, 'pump-dale' may come from ODan. *dāla* (cf. OIcel. *dæla*, s.f. 'a small dale; contrivance to serve the purpose of a ship's pump'; OIcel. *dallr* 'small tub'). The word was attested in Norman texts in the 14th century in the meaning of 'gutter-stone, sewer' (Bloch, s.v. *dalle*) and is widely used today in Normandy. The ON word must have first been used by the bilingual speakers of Neustria in the sense of 'pump', then 'sewer or apparatus for the flowing of water'; this developed into the meaning of 'hollow stone used as a sewer', then 'flat stone', as well as 'trough'. Fr. *dalot* 'pump' remains very close to the original ON word in meaning. Meyer-Lübke, in the *REW*

2460b, is justified in calling the development of the form *dæla* to *dalle* phonetically not understandable; an unmutated ODan. °*dāla* would explain the French word. Fr. *dalle* is also discussed by Dauzat, Bloch, Valkhoff, all s.v. *dalle*, Gamillscheg 288b, and Valkhoff, s.v. *dalle*, who cites *dêle* 'planche fixe' used 'at Liège of probable Middle Dutch origin, accepting W. von Wartburg's Norse etymology for the Norman forms. Cf. the *FEW*, III, 4b–5 for the Norman uses of the word.

18.   Fr. *dran*, OF *drenc*, s.m. 'drosse de basse vergue' (*DG*) < ON cf. OIcel. *dreng-r*, gen. *drengs*, s.m. 'boy; thick rope'. The word was first attested in Benoît de Sainte-Maure, a 12th century Norman writer. William the Conqueror used the word in the primary meaning in a letter cited by DuCange 'et quod ipsi in posterum vocarentur Drenges'; cf. Godefroy, s.v. *drench*, Cleasby-Vigfusson, s.v. *drengr*, but otherwise the word is attested in French only in the nautical sense. Brunot, I, 286–287, was mistaken when he stated that *drenc* is found in the Norman patois in the meaning of 'boy'. Fr. *dran* is also discussed by Dauzat, s.v. *dran*; *REW* 2768; Frahm, p. 63. Alessio, I, 63; and Sjögren, p. 405. The form *dronc* is found in the *Comptes du Clos des Galées de Rouen*, Delboulle, *Romania*, XXXIII (1904), 346, and in a note on the same page written by A. Thomas, it is stated that the word is identical with *drenc*, but the derivation from ON *þrøngva* 'to press' is not accurate; it was adopted by Meyer-Lübke, *REW*, 2nd ed., 8717, but in the 3rd ed. it was replaced by ON *dreng-r*, *REW* 2768. Cf. Tobler, s.v. *drenc*.

19.   *écarver*, v. tr. 'to scarf (two timbers)' < ON °*skarβa*, cf. Swedish *skarva* 'to join' (*DG*, Dauzat, s.v. *écarver*). The word was first attested in 1780, but the absence of preconsonantal [s] shows that the word is very old in the language; cf. also Sp. *escarba* 'joint'. Eng. *scarf* is also of ON origin (*OED*, s.v. *scarf*, sb. 2). The noun *écart*, s.m. 'amount of lap in joint' (a carpentry term) may be from ON °*skarf*, cf. Norw. *skarv* 'piece added to lengthen a board or garment' or may be derived from the verb *écarver*. The spelling of *écart* may have been influenced by that of Fr. *écart* 'distance apart, divergence'.

The noun *écart* was attested earlier than the verb, namely in 1752 (Dauzat, s.v. *écarver*).

20. *écoute*, s.f. 'sheet of sail'< ODan. **skout*, cf. OIcel. *skaut*, s.n. 'corner of a sail' (Bloch, Dauzat, Valkhoff, s.v. *écoute*; Falk, p. 96). OF *escote* is attested in Normandy in the 12th century (*Brut*, cf. Tobler, s.v. *escote*); the Dutch *schoot* proposed by the *REW* 7707, and Nyrop, *Wörter und Sachen*, VII (1921), 97, is not found in the nautical sense of the French word until the 16th century (Valkhoff, s.v. *écoute*). Fr. *écoutille*, s.f. 'hatchway' may be from Spanish *escotilla* (< OF *escoute*) according to Dauzat, s.v. *écoute* and Sandahl, p. 204. A derivative of *écoutille* is Fr. *écoutillon*, s.m. 'scuttle, booby-hatch'.

21. *équiper*, v. tr. 'to equip, fit out', originally 'to embark' in the 12th century. The modern sense does not appear until the 16th century. OIcel. *skipa* meant 'to fit out a ship' but may have meant 'to embark' as Norw. *skipe* does. The ON etymology is given by Falk-Torp, s.v. *skifte*, Hellquist, s.v. *skipa*, Kluge, s.v. *équipage*, and Gamillscheg 377a. Bloch and Dauzat give a Germanic source, while Bloch mentions ON *skipa* with some reservation. The *REW* 7997b gives AS *skipian* 'to embark' with no explanation of how the word reached the continent before the 12th century. The appearance of OF *eschiper* under a Norman-Picard form is another argument in favor of ON origin; if the word were older than the 10th century, [p] would not have remained. Cf. *équipage*, 15th c.; *équipe*, 1456; *équipée* 'prank' 1611; *équipement*, 1678; *équipier*.

22. OF *eschei*, *eschoi*, *escoi*, ONorm. *eskei*, s.m. 'type of ship'< ON cf. OIcel. *skeið*, gen. *skeiðar* 'war-ship, galley'. The word occurred in Wace's *Roman de Rou* (cf. Godefroy, s.v. *eschoi*) and is also discussed by Sjögren, p. 399; Hopfgarten, p. 24, and the *REW* 7988. The form *skeþ* appeared in runic Danish (Skautrup, I, 165). Compare OE *sceʒð* (with various alternate spellings) also from ON (Björkman, p. 36). For other examples, cf. Godefroy, III, 394b and Tobler, s.v. *escoi*. Cf. also Serjeantson, p. 64.

22b. OF *eschipe*, *esquipe*, s.f. 'ship', which the *REW* 7996 and Kemna, p. 141, derive from Frankish, may be from Old Danish, cf. OIcel. *skip*, s.n. 'ship'. The French word occurs in *La Chevalerie Ogier de Danemarche* in the 12th century (Tobler, s.v. *eschipe*).

23. OF *esneche*, ONorm. *esneque*, LL *snecka*, s.f. 'sorte de vaisseau léger, particulièrement employé par les pirates' (Godefroy, III, 503b)< ODan. *°snekkia* depalatalized form corresponding to OIcel. *snekkja,* gen. *snekkju,* s.f. 'a swift sailing ship' (Sjögren, p. 383). The word occurs in early Norman texts, including *La Chançun de Guillelme,* ed. Suchier, v. 215. The same word appears to have been applied to names of rocks in the northwestern Cotentin, *Longuesnèque* (Joret, p. 82). The Scandinavians probably brought the same word to Russia in the form ORuss. *shneka* (V. Thomsen, p. 129). The *REW* 8046 has an obvious misspelling of the ON form, where *snehha* is given instead of *°snekka;* this error appears in Tobler, s.v. *esnecke.* Other spellings are *esnesche, esnege, enesche, eneke(s), eneque,* and *esneke* (Tobler).

24. ONorm. *estague, étague, hutague, utage,* Fr. *itague,* s.f. 'tie'< ON cf. OIcel. *stag,* s.n. 'stay, esp. the rope from the mast to the stem'. The word occurred in the works of Wace and Benoît (Moisy, s.v. *utague*). The form *itague* would seem to be the same formation as OF *isnel* instead of *°esnel;* the forms with initial *u,* which are the earliest, offer difficulty. The ON *°uptaug* given by the *REW* 9075a would hardly explain the second syllable. For suggestions of derivation from Low German and Dutch, cf. Valkhoff, s.v. *itague.*

25. ONorm. *estiere,* s.f. 'rudder' in the *Lai d'Eliduc* of Marie de France (but given by Godefroy, *Lexique,* as a masculine noun) did not come directly from ON cf. OIcel. *stýri* as stated by Valkhoff, s.v. *estiere;* Falk, p. 73, Frahm, p. 57, and Nyrop, *Wörter und Sachen,* VII (1921), 97. An ODan. *°stiuri* better explains the diphthong in the French word. Compare *Dieppe,* Norman *tierre, mielle,* ONorm. PN *Bier,* etc. which are all from Old Danish words with the diphthong [iu] stressed on the first vowel. The word *estière* was listed in the *REW,* 2nd ed., 8338, but seems to have been omitted from the third edition of that work. Tobler, s.v. *estiere,* also cites the ON etymology.

26. Nautical Fr. *étui* in the expression *bonnette en étui* 'studding sail', OF *estoinc, estuinc, estuins,* s.m. in the *Roman de Brut* (Tobler, s.v. *estoinc*). 18th century Fr. *étouine* < ON *stǽðing-r,* s.m. 'braces', a naut. term. The word is discussed by A. Thomas, *Mélanges,* p. 99; Falk, p. 60, and Nyrop, *Wörter und Sachen,* VII (1921), 97. The most recent French form *étui* seems to have been influenced by *étui* 'case, box, cover' in expressions such as *étui de voile* 'sail cover' and *étui d'embarcation* 'boat cover'. Cf. also the *REW* 8273a.

27. ONorm. *estrenc, estran, estrems, estrens,* s.m. 'rope, cable' < ON, cf. OIcel. *streng-r,* appeared in Wace's *Roman de Brut* (cf. Godefroy, III, 641b and Tobler, s.v. *estrenc*). The word was treated by Nyrop, *Wörter und Sachen,* VII (1921), 97; Hopfgarten, p. 24; the *REW* 8297; Frahm, p. 68, Falk, p. 80; and Moisy, *Glossaire,* s.v. *estran,* as well as A. Thomas, *Romania,* XXIX (1900), 174.

28. *étambot,* s.m. 'stern-post', OF *estambot, estambor* (1596, Bloch) for *°estambord* < ON *°stafn-borð,* which has never been attested in the later Scandinavian literatures, but must have existed, as the two elements *stafn* and *borð* did. ON [v] written *f* in Old Icelandic may have already been nasalized when followed by [n] at the time of the settlement of Neustria; cf. Middle English *stam* of ON origin, Sandahl. Fr. *étambot* is discussed by Saggau, pp. 23–24; Dauzat, Bloch, s.v. *étambot;* cf. the *REW* 8215 where the ON word is given as an unstarred form, and the *DG,* where the second element is described as not clear.

29. *étambrai,* s.m. 'mast-hole' seems to be from ON *stafn* as far as the first element is concerned (*DG*); since one of the older meanings of the word is 'toile goudronnée' the second element must be Fr. *brai* 'tar' also of ON origin. Cf. above, § 11.

30. *étrave,* s.f. 'stem, stem-post', also *étable, étante, étauve, établure, estante* (Saggau, p. 18) < ON, cf. OIcel. *stafn,* s.m. 'stem of ship'. The Fr. word was attested in 1573 from an earlier *°estavre* < *°estavne* < ON *stafn;* another development was ON *stafn* > *estavne* > *°estavle* > *étable* and *étauve* (Bloch, s.v. *étrave*). A similar phonetic development took place in Fr.

havre and *hable,* OF *havene* (< ODan. *°hafn,* cf. OIcel. *höfn*).
The word is also treated by the *REW* 8214; the *DG,* s.v. *étrave;*
Alessio, I, 319, and Dauzat, s.v. *étrave.*

The form *estrible* occurring in the *Comptes du Clos des
galées de Rouen* in 1382 is, according to A. Thomas, a probable
variant of *étrave* or *étable.* Cf. Thomas, *Romania,* XXXIII (1904),
355, n. 3.

31.   AN *farcoste,* s.f. 'sort of ship' may be from ON, cf.
OIcel. *farkost-r,* s.m. 'a vessel, a ship', but W. von Wartburg
gives preference to Middle English *farcost* (*FEW,* III, 416a).
It is possible that the word was part of the Norman vocabulary
before 1066. Cf. the *OED,* s.v. *farcost,* of ON origin, attested in
1284.

32.   ONorm., OF *feste,* s.f. 'type of rope'< ON cf. OIcel.
fest-r, gen. *festar,* s.f. 'rope, cord, cable'. Of the two Norman
examples given by Godefroy (III, 770c) the earlier is from 1415.
The word also is found in the *Coutumier de la Vicomté de
l'Eau de Rouen,* cited by Moisy, *Glossaire,* s.v. *feste,* and Sjögren,
Romania, LIV (1928), 404. The form *fete* is found in Benoît's
Chronique des ducs de Normandie (Moisy). The form survives in Normandy in the verb *enfétonner,* listed by Moisy,
Glossaire, with the meaning of 'disposer un ensemble de cordes
et de sangles autour du corps des vaches, des boeufs, etc.
pâturant dans les vergers, pour les empêcher de relever la
tête et de manger les fruits pendant aux arbres'. The *FEW,*
III, 485a also gives Pont-Audemer *fétonner* 'se donner beaucoup de movement pour peu de besogne' and the noun *fétonnier*
'(cheval) attelé qui piétine et ne veut pas rester en place'; Le
Havre *être en féton* 'dans l'inquiétude'; Pont-Audemer *fétonnage*
'action de fétonner'; also *fétonnerie.* The word is also treated
by Nyrop, *Wörter und Sachen,* VII (1921), 97, and the *REW*
3267a.

33.   *flotte,* s.f. 'fleet' is from ON *floti,* s.m. 'float, raft,
fleet'. Both meanings of the ON word appeared in French:
ONorm. *flotte* 'fleet' in the *Chançun de Guillelme,* 1080, and OF
a flotte 'en radeau' ca. 1260, corresponding exactly to ON *a
floti* 'afloat' from ON *flot* 'floating'. Cf. also *flotte de marrein*
'raft', Cotgrave; Fr. *flotte* 'train de bois flotté'; MFr. *floton*

'raft', 16th c.; Fr. *flotter* (du bois), also *flottement, flottaison, flottage, flotteur, flottable, flottabilité*. The ON word became part of the Romance of Neustria and passed to Bordeaux where early examples of the word are found, and then to Iberia. ME *flote* 'fleet', 1275, is from French or Norse, AS *flota* having had the meaning of 'float' only. For a complete discussion of Fr. *flotte*, see Sjögren, 388–9 and the *FEW*, III, 640.

34. *guindas, guindeau*, s.m. 'windlass' is from ON *vindáss*, s.m. 'windlass'. The form *windas* occurred in Wace's *Roman de Rou*, 12th c. The form *vindas*, which Falk, p. 81, n. 1 thought to be a loan from Dutch, is the Norman form showing the change [w] to [v], whereas *guindas* is the central French form, which shows that the word must have passed early from Normandy to Paris in the form *windas* to become [gwindas]. The word *guindeau* is a contamination of *guindas* with words in -*eau* when the meaning of the element -*as* was no longer understood; cf. *havenet, haveneau*, §92. A similar contamination was responsible for *guindal* 'treuil', probably a back-formation of the plural form *guindeaux*. Cf. also *vindau* alongside of *vindas* 'giant stride'. The word is also treated in the *DG*, s.v. *guindas*; *OED*, s.v. *windlass*; Dauzat, s.v. *guinder*; Brunot, I, 287 and Saggau, p. 129.

35. *guinder*, v. tr. 'to hoist, raise with a windlass' from ON *vinda* 'to wind, hoist by means of a windlass', first appeared in Wace, *Roman de Brut* in the 12th c. and in the *Vie de St. Gilles*. ONorm. *winder* passed early into Central French, becoming *gwinder when [gw-] was considered a variant of Norm. [w-]. Derived forms: *guindelle* 'sorte de bateau' 1521–31; *guinderesse*, s.f. 'mast-rope' 1606; *guindant*, s.m. 'hoist of sail' 1690; *guindre*, s.f. 'a reel, or wheel to wind silk on' (Cotgrave) in Olivier de Serres (cf. Huguet); *guinde*, s.f. 'petite presse à moulinet, dite aussi *guindas*, pour catir à froid les étoffes de laine'; *guindage, guindaige*, s.m. 'hoisting', 1517 (*DG*, Huguet); used figuratively in *guinder ses manières* 'to effect a stiff, starched manner' and *se guinder* 'to affect a lofty manner' in Molière; cf. Fénelon's phrase *un style guindé* (*DG*).

36. Norm. *hammer* (patois of Le Havre) 'to row so as to make the boat move backwards' seems to be from ON, cf. OIcel.

hamla 'to backwater' and OSwed. *hamna,* ODan. *hafnæ* with similar meanings. (P. Barbier, *RLiR,* X (1934), 125–6).

37. *hauban,* OF *hobent, hoban, hobenc,* s.m. 'shroud' is probably from an ODan. *°hafuð-benda,* cf. OIcel. *hǫfuð-benda,* s.f. 'stay, shroud'. The word appears in Norman authors in the 12th c., and is treated by Falk, p. 59; Bloch, Dauzat, Valkhoff and Frahm, p. 60. The *REW* 4155 gives a Dutch source, but Valkhoff states that Middle Dutch *hobant* is only attested in the sense of 'diadem' and the Dutch word does not have the meaning of the Fr. word until recent times. Derived forms: *hauban(n)er,* v. tr. 'to guy, stay, brace', 1690; *hauban(n)age,* s.m. 'guying'; *galhauban, cale-hauban, galauban, galeban,* s.m. 'backstay' (*DG*).

38. ONorm. *hel,* s.m. 'barre du gouvernail' seems to be from an ODan. *°helm,* an unbroken form corresponding to OIcel. *hjalm,* s.m. 'rudder'. ONorm. *hel* appears in Wace's *Roman de Brut,* and the possibility of the ON origin of the word was seen by A. Thomas, *Romania,* XLIV (1918), 348. For the disappearance of [m], cf. ODan. *Rolf*> ONorm. *°Rol*> ONorm. *Rou,* with the Lat. form *Rollo* based on *°Rol.*

39. *hublot,* OF *huvelot,* s.m. 'port hole' first attested in Rouen in 1382 is derived from OF *huve* 'sorte de coiffure' (Bloch), but this may be from ON *húfa* 'cap, bonnet', although other sources are given in the etymological dictionaries. Bloch, Dauzat, s.v. *hublot* and Barbier, *RLiR,* X (1934), 153–7 trace the word to a West Germanic source, whereas the *REW* 4166 gives AS *hol* as the etymon.

40. *hune* s.f. 'top' (naut.) is from ON *hún-n,* s.m. 'knob at the top of the mast-head'. The word first appeared in *La Vie de St. Gilles* in the 12th c., and the derived form *hunier,* s.m. 'topsail' has been used since the 17th c. (Bloch, Dauzat, *DG, REW* 4240, Saggau, p. 67, Frahm, p. 61 and Falk, p. 59). By extension, *hune* also has the meaning of 'grosse poutre terminée par deux tourillons et à laquelle une cloche est suspendue' (*DG*). From this use of *hune* a further development to 'head' took place in some areas of Normandy (Sjögren, p. 393). From *heune,* s.f. 'head' is derived Norm. *heunas, heumas, heumat* 'stubborn' (listed by Du Bois and Duméril).

41. *jaumière*, s.f. 'rudder hole' is derived from OF *jaume* 'rudder' (< ON *hjálm*, s.m. 'helm, rudder'). The Fr. word is first attested in Thomas Corneille, 1694 (*DG*, s.v. *jaumière*). The ON etymology is also given by Falk, p. 75 and Nyrop, *Wörter und Sachen*, VII (1921), 97.

42. *liban*, s.m. 'upper and lower bolt ropes of a large net', in a Latinized form in 1363 (Ducange), appeared in 1769 in Duhamel du Monceau, and may be related to ON *lík-band*, s.n. 'leech-band, winding sheet' (cf. Eng. *leech* of ON origin). According to Barbier, *Miscellanea Lexicographica*, XXIII (1942) 309 ff., OF *liban* may well have been used in Normandy in the sense of 'leech-rope'; its first element is found in ONorm. *lisprot*, *lispreu* 'extérieur des voiles' found in Wace.

43. *ouaiche, ouage, houache, houage*, s.f. 'sillage d'un vaisseau', first used by Guillet in 1678, admitted by the Academy in 1762 (*DG*) seems to come from ON *vǫk*, gen. *vakar*, s.f. 'hole, opening in the ice'. For the *ai*, cf. *avantaige* for *avantage*, and for the forms with *g*, cf. *esnege* for *esneche*, §23. The phonetic development of ON *vǫk*, proposed by the *DG*, has not been adequately explained, but cf. Eng. *wake* 'track left by ship on water' also of ON origin (*OED*, s.v. *wake*, sb.)

44. *quille*, s.f. 'keel', first attested in 1382 in a Rouen text (Bloch, Dauzat, *FEW*, II, 726) seems to come from ON *kilir*, pl. of *kjǫl-r*, s.m. 'keel'. Dutch *kiel* accepted as the etymon by Saggau, p. 13, Valkhoff, s.v. *quille*, Gamillscheg 730b, *REW* 4698 and Dauzat did not appear until the 16th c. with the meaning 'keel' (Bloch, Valkhoff). Falk, p. 34 states that the ON word entered French through the intermediary of Dutch; this is not likely in view of the appearance of the French word several centuries earlier than the Dutch word; however, Dutch had another word *kiel* like AS *céol* meaning 'ship'. The ON etymology given by Bloch and the *FEW*, II, 726 seems most acceptable; Eng. *keel* is also of ON origin. The *FEW* explains the palatalization in *quille* as due to the [i] in the ON plural *kilir* and in the dative *kili*. Among the derived forms given by the *FEW* are: Jersey *chelle* 'keel'; *quillé*, adj. 'provided with a keel', 1845; *quillage*, s.m. 'keelage dues' 1472, now archaic; *équille*, s.f. 'extrémité de l'éperon d'une galère, qui est fixé

sur le bout de la quille'; Parisian *s'enquiller* 's'embaucher'. Cf. Sjögren, pp. 395–7 for a detailed study of Fr. *quille*.

45.　*raguer*, v. tr. 'to chafe, rub (a rope)' may be from ON *raka* 'to sweep away, rake, shave'. Barbier, *Miscellanea Lexicographica*, XX (1939), 86 states that Norw. *rage* explains the word best; a similar etymology is given by Gamillscheg 736. However, *raguer*, attested since the 17th c. could very well be from ON *raka*, since voicing of [-k-] was common in Normandy. The *DG* and the *REW* 7006 derive our word from Eng. *rag*, whereas Dauzat and Valkhoff trace the word to Dutch.

46.　ONorm. *raque*, s.f. 'boule percée servant à faire un racage', first attested in the *Comptes du clos des galées de Rouen*, 1382 is from ON *rakki*, s.m. 'parrel' (*DG*, Sjögren, 389–390, Barbier, *RLR*, LXV (1927), 33). Fr. *rague*, cited by Barbier shows the Norm. voicing of [-k-]. A derived form is *racage*, s.m. 'parrel', 1634 (*DG*).

47.　*riper*, v. tr. 'to scrape, polish (stone); to let slip (the chain on capstan)'; v.i. 'to scrape, rub, skid', attested in 1328, admitted by the Academy 1835, may be from ON *rispa* 'to scratch'. However Dauzat, the *DG* and the *REW* 7334a give as the origin the German dial. *rippen* (cf. German *reiben* 'to rub').

48.　*ris*, s.m. 'reef (in sail)' in Wace, 12th c., probably a plural of earlier *rif* (< ON *rif*, s.n. 'reef'). The word is treated by Bloch, Dauzat, Saggau, p. 82, *DG* and Frahm, p. 65. Cf. Eng. *reef* also from ON *rif* (*OED*, s.v. reef, sb. 1). Der.: *arriser*, v. tr. & i. 'to touch (a sail)', 1643.

49.　OF *run* 'fond de cale', 1386 (Bloch, s.v. *arrimer*) is from ON *rúm*, s.n. 'room, room in a ship'. The word survives in Normandy as: *arrun*, s.m. 'arrangement, order' (Maze, patois of Le Havre); *arruner*, v. tr. 'arranger' (Duméril, Du Bois), cf. OF *arruner* in Cotgrave 'to rank, sort, range . . . .'; Norm. *areuner* 'mettre en route' with Norm. change from [y] to [œ]; *déruner* 'déplacer, déranger'; *derumaïr* 'déranger' (Guernsey) cf. Métivier, *ALF Supplément* I, 63c; *r'aruner* 'remettre en ordre' (Rouen, 17th c., D. Ferrand, V, 196); *rum, run*, s.m. 'place' (Guernsey); *run*, s.n. 'rang' (Le Havre). OF *arumer* 'ranger la cargaison dans la cale' 1386–1798 (Bloch, s.v. *arrimer*).

50. ONorm., OF *sigle*, s.m. & f. 'sail' is from ON *sigla*, s.f. 'mast', perhaps crossed with ON *segl*, s.n. 'sail' or with influence of OF *sigler* 'to sail' (< ON *sigla*). Sjögren, p. 383 has suggested that OF *sigle*, which appeared in Wace and in the *Vie de St. Alexis*, was used with both genders because of the synonym *voile*, also of both genders.

51. *sombrer*, v.i. 'to founder, sink', attested since 1680 (Bloch) may be from ON *sumla* 'to be flooded'. The statement in the *DG* that ON *sumbla* 'to throw in a disorderly fashion' (which semantically does not explain the word as well as ON *sumla*) is not the etymon for phonetic reasons is not accurate; ON [ŭ] was normally treated as OF [o]. For the change from [l] to [r], cf. *havre, hable* and *étrave, étable* where [r] has become [l]. The ON source is given by Gamillscheg, 807a; Bloch and Dauzat express doubt about the Scandinavian source of *sombrer*, as does the *DG*.

52. *tanguer*, v.i. 'to pitch'; Norman *tanguer* 'to stop a leak'. Paul Barbier, *Miscellanea Lexicographica*, XX (1939), 99 ff., states that French *tanguer* originally meant 'to prick, to pierce' as in Berrichon *tanguer* 'to strike, to ill-treat', and OF *tangonner* 'to prick'; for the semantic development cf. Fr. *piquer* in the expression *piquer une tête dans l'eau* 'to plunge headlong'. The word is related to OF *tangre* 'tang of a knife'; the more normal *tangue* which must have meant 'tang of a knife' is found in Normandy as 'spit, or long narrow strip of sea sand'. Both of these meanings are found in ON, cf. OIcel. *tangi*, s.m. 'a point projecting into the sea; the pointed end by which the blade is driven into the handle'. The ON dative plural *tanganum* could easily have given *tangre* through an original ONorm. *°tangne;* cf. ONorm. *havene* > *havre*. The ON etymology is also found in the *REW* 8559; Joret, *Romania*, IX (1880), 303, n. 2. Dauzat and Bloch give a Frisian source. The word in question was first attested in 1680 as *tanquer* (*DG*); Bloch gives 1678; in 1694, Thomas Corneille used *un navire qui tangue* showing a common Norman hesitation between [nk] and [ng]. The *DG*, s.v. *tanguer* would have derived the word from Norman *tangue* 'slimy sea-sand' but for the fact that *tanquer* was the first attested form; of course, *tangue* is a dif-

ferent word (see below §166). For the Norman unvoicing of certain intervocalic consonants, cf. Norm. *rocu*, Fr. *rogué* 'roed'.

53. ONorm. *tialz*, s.m. 'tente dressée sur un navire au repos suivant l'usage scandinave' (Godefroy, *Lexique*)< ON, cf. OIcel. *tjald*, s.n. 'tent, on land or on ships, esp. when in harbor'. The French word has the nominative singular and accusative plural ending -s, and seems to represent °*tialts*. The etymology is given by Frahm, p. 66, who quotes an example of the word used in *La Vie de St. Gilles*. Viggo Brøndal, *Substrater og Laan i Romansk og Germansk*, pp. 136 ff., seems unjust in his skepticism about the ON etymology; that ONorm. *tialz* presupposes an older °*tēlds* because *biaus*< *bellus* seems totally unnecessary, in view of the fact that ON *tjald* became integrated in the Romance of Neustria as °*tialt*, with the plural *tialz*, and thus had no history in France before 900.

54. OF *tille*, s.f. 'compartiment à l'avant et à l'arrière, servant d'armoire à l'équipage' (Godefroy, X, 766c, Sjögren, p. 384); Fr. *tille*, s.f. 'cuddy of half-decked boat', 'petit compartiment réservé à l'avant et à l'arrière d'une barque, pour serrer les objets de ceux qui la montent' (*Grand Dictionnaire Larousse*, cited by Sjögren, p. 384). The word is from ON, cf. OIcel. *þilja*, s.f. 'plank', pl. *þiljur* 'the deck'. The DG gives the first example as 1702, in Aubin's *Dictionnaire de marine*.

54b. *tillac*, s.m. 'deck' attested in Rouen in 1382 (*DG*) is also from ON, cf. OIcel. *þilja*, with an unexplained suffix. The ON etymology for *tillac* is found in the DG, Saggau, Dauzat; Bloch; *REW* 8708; Falk, p. 48; and Sandahl, p. 166.

55. *tolet, toulet, touret*, s.m. 'thole-pin' appeared first in Cotgrave as *tollet* (1611) from an ONorm. °*tol*< ON, cf. OIcel. *þoll-r*, s.m. 'fir-tree, thole, wooden peg'; cf. also English *thole*. The word is treated by the *REW* 8710; Dauzat, Bloch, DG, s.v. *tolet*, and Falk, p. 71; *toletière*, s.f. 'the strengthening plate on the gunwale to receive the rowlock; rowlock'.

56. *touer*, v. tr. 'to tow'< ON, cf. OIcel. *toga* 'to draw, pull, stretch' (Dauzat, Bloch, DG, s.v. *touer*). The noun *touage* was attested first in the 13th century. Derived forms: *touage*, s.m. 'towing', 13th c.; *touée*, s.f. 'câble pour touer', attested as *thouée* in 1415 (*DG*); *toue*, s.f. 'flat-bottomed river-barge' in

Cotgrave as *touë*; *toueur, toueuse*, s.m. & f. 'ancre de toue, remor-
queur pour touer', attested in 1643 as *toïeus* (*DG*); *toueur*,
adj. 'warping' in *ancre toueuse*; *toueur*, s.m. 'warper'.

57. *tribord*, s.m. 'starboard', *estribord* in 1528, used by
Rabelais in 1552, probably a Norman word in origin (Sainéan,
La Langue de Rabelais, I, 107) may be from an ODan. °*stiorborð*
(cf. OIcel. *stjórnborði* 'starboard'), which must have given
ONorm. °*estierebord*, with reduction of the diphthong to °*es-
tirbord*, and then through metathesis, *estribord*. Cf. ONorm.
estiere (< ODan. °*stiūri*, OIcel. *stýri* 'rudder'). The ON source
is given by the *DG* and Frahm, p. 58; the *REW* 8341, Alessio,
I, 321 and Gamillscheg 864 give the impression that *tribord*
is a recent loan from Dan. *styrbord*, which according to Falk-
Torp has its form from Low German, the native ON word
being *stjórnborði*.

58. *varangue*, s.f. 'floor timber, floor frame', first attested
in Rouen in 1385 (*DG*) is from ODan. *vrang*, adj. 'bent, curved'
but probably also a noun 'rib in a ship' (cf. OIcel. *rǫng* and
ME *wrong, wrang* of ON origin, Sandahl. s.v. *wrong* and AS
wranga 'hold of a ship', Serjeantson, p. 72). Fr. *varangue* has
an anaptyctic vowel (cf. *canif, harousse, canart*). For a discussion of the word, see Sjögren, p. 390, *REW* 9574, Falk, p. 46.

59. *vibord*, s.m. 'sheer-strake of a ship'< ON °*vígi-borð*
(cf. ON *vígi*, s.n. 'bulwarks or gunwale of ship', *borð*, s.n. 'board,
plank, side of ship', first used by Furetière, 1690 (*DG*, Dauzat,
Falk, p. 14, *REW* 9537).

The Sea

60. OF *brin*, s.m. 'bruit, jouissance, orgueil', probably
from ONorm. °*brin* 'noise of the waves', from ON *brim*, s.n.
'surf' (*FEW*, I, 527b; Sjögren, p. 399; *REW*, 2nd ed. 1301). But
cf. P. Barbier, *Miscellanea Lexicographica*, IX (1932), 60–61
for a theory of West Germanic origin.

61. ONorm. *diep*, s.m. 'channel' 140a, 1526, cited by Delboulle, *Romania*, XXXIII (1904), 345 seems to be from ODan.
°*diūpt*, cf. OIcel. *dýpt* 'depth'. Cf. *FEW*, III, 198a. *Dieppe*

seems to be from the same source. *Dieppedalle* seems to contain
the adjective, ODan. *diūp* (cf. OIcel. *djúp-r*) and *dal-r* 'dale'.

62.   *flot*, s.m. 'wave'< ON *flóð* 'flood' (*FEW*, III, 626b) or
ON *flot* 'floating' (Sjögren, p. 400). OF *fluet* of West Germanic
origin is a different word, and the fact that OF *flot* and *fluet*
existed side by side in the 12th c. makes the theory that *fluet* became *flot* through influence of Fr. *flotter* unlikely (Sjögren). OF
flot, first attested in Wace, existed originally in Normandy, while
fluet was confined to eastern and north-eastern France; AN
fluet was probably of Picard origin. Among the additional
forms given by the *FEW* are: Jersey *fllot*, Pont-Audemer *flot*
'marée montante'; Fr. *reflot* 'reflux de la mer' 1515–1622; and
Norm. *flouée*, s.f. 'marée' (Rouen, 1604). Cf. also *reflotter* 'refluer', *renflouer* 'remettre à flot', *renflouement, renflouage* 'action de renflouer', *afflouer* 'to refloat', *afflouage, afflouement*
'refloating of stranded vessel'. The word *flot* seems to be losing
ground and is being replaced in many compounds by forms of
Fr. *flux*. Cf. *reflux* for older *reflot*, and *refluer* for older *reflotter*.
Many similar compounds have been made from both the Norse
and the Latin root: cf. MFr. *contre-flot* and archaic Fr. *contre-
flus* 'marées venant de front l'une contre l'autre', the latter in the
FEW, III, 646a, s.v. *fluxus*. It is to be noted that Fr. *flot* has
both the meaning of 'wave' and that of 'floating' which may
even be an indication that ON *flot* 'floating' and ON *flóð* 'flood'
were both integrated in the Romance of Neustria. See also
above, §33.

62a.   *gare*, s.f. 'siding (of river, canal)' is according to
Falk, p. 25, from ON cf. OIcel. *vǫrr*, s.f. 'fenced-in landing
place'. This etymology which is phonetically and semantically
sound, has been accepted by Skautrup, I, 104, and the *REW*
9501. Gamillscheg, 459a criticizes it on account of the late appearance of *gare* in French; the 15th century does not seem
late, however, when we consider that Fr. *écarver* was not attested until the 18th century (see above, §19). Dauzat, s.v.
gare derives this from Frankish *warôn*; Bloch, s.v. *gare* also
derives it from Frankish, while the *DG* derives it from the verb
garer, which it considers another form of *guérir*.

63.   Norman *grune*, s.f. 'bas-fond, fond rocailleux' (Sjögren, p. 393); Jersey *grune*, s.f. 'rocher' (*Glossaire du patois jersiais*, s.v. *grune*); Guernsey *grœn*, s.f. 'fond rocailleux' (Métivier, s.v. *grune; ALF Supplément*, I, 197, s.v. *roche;* and Sjögren, p. 393) < ODan. *°grūnn;* cf. OIcel. *grúnn-r*, gen. *grúnns*, s.m. 'bottom (of sea or water)'. The element is common in the toponymy of the Cotentin peninsula: *La Grune, La Grunette, les Grunes*, etc. (Longnon, p. 285). Other examples are given by Joret, p. 85, n. 3. The ON word is only listed with a short vowel; we must presume an ODan. etymon with long [u].

64.   *havre*, s.m. 'port, harbor', OF *havene, hafne, havne* (Godefroy, IX, 715a), also *able, hable*, LL *hablum, haula* (Du Cange, III, 609a, 635a) has been attested since the twelfth century. ON *hǫfn*, gen. *hafnar*, s.f. 'haven, harbor' has been rejected by Valkhoff, s.v. *havre* because of the ON vowel; but the ODan. form was *°hafn*. The *REW* 3982 gives a Low German etymology, while Bloch, s.v. *havre* derives it from Middle Dutch and Middle English. Note that Kluge, s.v. *Hafen*, derives AS *haefene* from ON *hǫfn*. Cf. E. Binet, "La jetter dans un hable, ou havre ou plage, qui est un bord de mer sans fond" (Huguet, s.v. *hable*).

65.   OF *lagan, laguen, lagand*, s.m. 'débris d'un vaisseau que la mer jette sur le rivage, épave; droit qui autorisait, au profit du seigneur de tout territoire maritime, la saisie des choses apportées par la mer ou échouées sur les côtes; destruction, ruine, dégât'. By extension in expressions such as *aller au lagan* 'aller à sa ruine', the word acquired the meaning of 'consommation excessive, profusion; abondance, quantité' (Godefroy, *Lexique*). The word seems to come from ODan. *°lagn* with the same meaning as OIcel. *lǫgn*, pl. *lagnir*, s.f. 'a net laid in the sea' which in Normandy must have acquired the sense of 'goods or wreckage lying on the bed of the sea'. The ON etymology is given by the *OED*, s.v. *lagan* and Frahm, p. 92. Hopfgarten, p. 50, sees in *lagan* ON *lǫg* 'law' (which is acceptable as far as the vowel is concerned since ODan. *°lag* > Eng. *law*); there may have been contamination with ON *lǫg* 'law' which survived for a time in Normandy as *lage* 'law' (see Moisy, *Glossaire*, s.v. *lage*, and cf. below). However, it seems that

'maritime law' was not the original meaning of Fr. *lagan* but a result of a semantic development from the concept of 'wreck' to 'law governing maritime wrecks'. The ending -*an* is not clear; cf. ODan. *rogn*> Fr. *rogue*, §100.

66.   *Quillebeuf* (S.-I.) may have as its first element ON, cf. OIcel. *kíl-l* s.m. 'narrow inlet, canal' or ON, cf. OIcel. *kelda*, s.f. 'well, spring'; the latter is the etymology given by Longnon, p. 282. ON *kíl-l* is phonetically and semantically more suitable; however, ODan. had a palatalized [ld] which could account for *Quille*-; cf. ON *telgja*> Fr. *tille* 'hachette de couvreur'.

67.   *ras, raz*, s.m. 'strong current (in isthmus or estuary)' < ON *rás*, s.f. 'course, channel' (cf. English *race*< ON, cf. OIcel *rás*, *OED*, s.v. *race* sb. 1). The word, which is first attested in the 15th c. (*DG*, s.v. *raz*) may have passed from Norse to Norman to Breton and then to French, as the spelling *raz* may indicate. The word is treated by the *DG* and Dauzat, where a Breton origin is given, and by Bloch whose etymology is followed here.

68.   *sonde*, s.f. 'sounding-lead', first attested in the 12th c. (*DG*, Bloch) may be from ON *sund*, s.n. 'sound, strait, swimming'. The *REW* 8406 traces the word to Lat. *subundare*, but cf. the *OED* s.v. *sound*. sb. 1, 4 where it is stated that the ON word seems to have played a part in the development of the Eng. word. The place-name *Le Sund* [sõ:d] off the Norman coast retains an earlier spelling and seems to be from the same ON word. The derived forms are: *sondage*, s.m. 'sounding', 1769; *sonder*, v. tr. 'to sound, examine', attested in Rouen in 1382 (cf. *sonder* 'to sound' speaking of a whale, which seems to recall the meaning 'swimming' of ON *sund*); *sondeur*, s.m. 'leadsman', Furetière, 17th c., also 'sounding-apparatus'; *sondeuse*, s.f. 'borer'; *insondable*, adj. 'unsoundable', 1578; *insondé*, adj. 'unfathomed'.

69.   *vague*, s.f., ONorm. *wages* (*Tristan*, 12th c. and Wace, *Roman de Brut*) is from ON *vág-r*, gen. *vágs*, s.m. 'wave, sea, creek, bay' (Bloch, Dauzat, *REW* 9477, Sjögren, p. 392). Cf. OF *vaguier*, v.i. 'faire des vagues' (Godefroy) and Fr. *vagueux*, adj. 'covered with waves, choppy'.

70. *varec*(*h*), s.m. 'wrack, seaweed', ONorm. *warec*, 1181 'wreck', ONorm. 14th c. 'seaweed', is from ODan. °*vrek*(*i*) (cf. OIcel. *reki*, s.m. 'a thing drifted ashore'). Cf. Eng. *wreck*, from AN *wrec*(*h*) of ON origin (*OED*, s.v. *wreck*, sb.). The meaning 'wreck' is now obsolete in French; the shift in meaning from 'thing drifted ashore' to 'seaweed drifted ashore' is slight. The form *vrek* survives at Guernsey (*ALF Supplément*, I, 228c) and at Jersey two derivatives exist: *vraicquir*, v.i. 'ramasser ou couper du varech' and *vraicqueurs*, s.m. 'ceux qui ramassent le varech'. The ON etymology of *varech* is in the *DG* and Bloch; the statement in Alessio, I, 168 and Dauzat that *varech* is of AS origin shows a disregard for the material in the *OED*.

71. Norm. *vâtre*, s.f. 'eau bourbeuse, fange, boue' (Moisy, *Glossaire*) may be from ON *vatr*, a rare and early form of ON *vatn*, gen. *vatns*, s.n. 'water'.

72. -*vic* in *Sanvic*, S.-I. and in *Cap-Levy*, *Kapelvic* in the 12th c. seems to be from ON *vík* 'inlet, small bay'. The first element of *Sanvic* is probably ON *sand-r*, s.m. 'sand'. (Cf. Longnon, p. 291).

73. AN *waif*, *wayf*, ONorm. *gaif*, *gayf*, s.m. 'chose que personne ne réclame', adj. 'perdu, que personne ne réclame' are according to the *OED*, s.v. *waif* from ON *veif* 'something flapping or waving'. The word appears in the LL of Normandy as *vaiva* and *gaiva* (*Coutumiers de Normandie*, ed. Ernest-Joseph Tardif, II, 50). Cf. the derived forms *gaivage*, s.m. 'droit de s'emparer des animaux et des objets dont les maîtres étaient inconnus . . . .', *gaivement*, s.m: 'délaissement fait pour un an . . . et qui tient lieu du payement des profits', *gaiver*, v. tr. 'céder . . . au seigneur censier l'exploitation . . . de la maison . . . .' (Godefroy, *Lexique*).

Names of Fishes and Fishing Terms

74. Archaic Fr. *aumées*, s.f. pl., *hamaux*, s.m. pl. 'names of the two outer nets of the trammel' are from ON *ham-r*, gen. *hams*, s.m. 'skin, slough', according to P. Barbier, *Mis-*

cellanea Lexicographica, XXV (1944), 54–55. First attested in Isambert, 1681, the words go back to ONorm. °*ham* with a diminutive ending -*el*; *hamaux* is then the plural of °*hamel*, and *aumées* shows the Norm. change of [a] to the diphthong written *au*, and is really the diminutive °*aumets* developed from °*hamets*, another diminutive of unattested ONorm. °*ham*. Cf. Dutch *haam* and German *Hamen* which are also net names.

75. Norm. *baite, bète, béque*, s.f. 'bait' are from ON *beita*, s.f. 'bait' (*FEW*, I, 316a) with the derivatives *bété* (Bessin) 'amorcer', Guernsey *bétaïr* 'amorcer un hameçon ou un piège', Norm. *abéter, abéti, abecté* 'amorcer', Archaic Fr. *abet* 'appât pour les poissons', and Norm. *abet* 'appât'.

76. Fr. *célerin*, Norm. *célin, seltã*, ONorm. *selletan*, Pic. *célan, scellan*, Fr. *scélan*, s.m. 'sorte de poisson qui a de la ressemblance avec le hareng et qui sert à faire des appâts' are from ON *sild* or *sild*. The words are discussed in detail by P. Barbier, *RLiR*, LII (1909), 124 and in the *RDR*, I (1909), 449; cf. also the *REW* 7910 and Dauzat, s.v. *célerin*. The word was first attested in the 13th c. as *harenc celerin*. The change of [i] to [e] has not been explained, but all factors point to ON origin; cf. Eng. *sile* of ON origin (*OED*, s.v. *sile*, sb. 2) and Russian, Lithuanian and Old Prussian words of ON origin (Hellquist, s.v. *sill*). Cf. also Finnish *silli* 'herring'.

77. OF *cole*, s.f. 'sorte de poisson' may be from Old Norse (cf. Swed. *kolja* 'haddock'). In the Scandinavian languages the word exists without the final element -*fish* of Dutch *koolvis(ch)* and Eng. *coalfish*. OF *cole* was attested in the 14th c., and Fr. *colin* seems to be derived from OF *cole* with influence of the proper name *Colin*.

78. Fr. *crabe*, s.m., Norm. *crabe*, s.f. 'crab' may be from ON *krabbi*, s.m. 'crab'. The fact that Norm. *crabe* is still feminine, the original gender of OF *crabe*, may mean that *crabe* was first used in Normandy; the masculine gender of *crabe* seems to be due to false derivation from Lat. *carabus* according to Sjögren, *Studia neophilologica*, I (1928), 125. Cf. *crabier*, s.m. 'nom spécifique de divers animaux qui se nourrissent de crabes'.

79. Norm. *dranet, drannet, drenet,* first attested in Thomas Corneille in 1694, seem to be from ON *drag-net* 'drag-net' rather than from Eng. *drag-net,* the latter source being in the *FEW,* III, 153b. P. Barbier, *RLiR,* X (1934), 99 ff. expresses skepticism concerning the alleged English origin of a word attested not only in the Channel Islands but also in the Bessin, at Bernières-sur-Mer, C. and at La Hague. Fr. *drainette* 'filet que l'on traîne à la dérive pour prendre le petit poisson' seems to be related to Norm. *dranet,* with influence of Fr. *drivenette,* according to the *FEW,* III, 153, n. 2. For other Norman words with the element *-net* (< ON *net,* s.n. 'net') cf. *havenet,* below, §92.

80. Fr. dialectal *écade* 'clupea alosa' Cuvier< ON °*skadd,* cf. OIcel. *skata* 'skate', Norw. *skadd* 'kleine Schnäpel'. The form of the French word shows that it goes back to at least the 12th century. Fr. *écade* is discussed by P. Barbier, *RLR,* LXV (1927), 11–13.

81. Norman *écore,* s.f. 'tally-sheet; *écorer,* v. tr. 'to keep tally of fish landed' (in Channel ports); *écoreur,* s.m. 'tally-keeper'; ONorm. *escorre,* v. tr. 'compter, supputer, marquer' in Benoît, *Chronique des ducs de Normandie,* cited by Moisy, *Glossaire,* s.v. *escorre* is from ON, cf. OIcel. *skora* 'to make an incision', and *skor* 'notch, incision'. Cf. English *score* also of ON origin. (Hellquist, s.v. *snes; OED,* s.v. *score*). The noun *écoreur* was first attested in 1708 (*DG*). The *DG* calls the verb *écorer* 'surveiller la vente du poisson' a neologism and derives it from English *score,* an etymology also found in Gamillscheg 340a. Phonetic chronology seems to have been completely disregarded by the *DG* and Gamillscheg, and *écorer* could hardly be called a neologism, since effacement of pre-consonantal [s] took place during the 11th, 12th and 13th centuries in France (Pope, p. 151).

82. Norman *s'écorer* 'to stay oneself, to support oneself' seems to be a different word from Norman *écorer* 'to keep tally of fish landed'. Norman *écorer* 'to support' is probably from an ON word corresponding to OIcel. *skorða* 'to prop, support' (cf. OIcel. *skorða,* s.f. 'stay, prop'). The Norman form occurs in Gustave Flaubert's *Madame Bovary* (New York, Charles Scrib-

ner's Sons, 1930), p. 206: ". . . et quand on lui donnait quelque gros ouvrage, il s'écorait dessus, préférablement". Cf. also p. 412, where the Norman word is defined by the editor.

83. *écrède*, s.f. 'écaille' (patois of Guernsey); cf. also Moisy, *Glossaire*, s.v. *écrède*, Métivier, s.v. *écrède*, as well as the *ALF*, *Supplément*, I, 67a, s.v. *écailles*, where the Guernsey form is given. The word seems to be related to ON *skreið*, s.f. 'shoal of fish, dried fish'.

84. Norm. *flie, flion* 'clam', first attested in 1558, seems to be of ON origin, cf. Dan. *fli* 'acorn', according to Gamillscheg and Dauzat, but this etymology is semantically difficult (*FEW*, III, 620b).

85. Norm. *flonde, flondre, fllandre*, s.f. 'flounder' is from ODan. *flundra* 'flounder' (*FEW*, III, 643b; *REW* 3389; Barbier, *RLR*, LI (1908), 396; Sjögren, p. 384). The earliest example of Norm. *flondre* seems to be from 1435 (Sjögren, p. 383, n. 1). Cf. Eng. *flounder* of ON origin (Falk-Torp, s.v. *flyndre*; Kluge, s.v. *Flunder*).

86. Norm. *guimoisson, guimoisseron* 'small salmon' in the patois of Avranches may be from ON *vima* 'giddiness, hesitation' presumably from the movements of the fish, through an unattested ONorm. *°guimois*, from an older *°guime*, according to Barbier, *Revue de philologie française*, XXXII (1918), 153.

87. *gord*, s.m. 'rang de perches en angle au fond d'une rivière fermé par un filet où le poisson vient se prendre' is of Norse origin, according to Nyrop, *Romania*, LV (1929), 602; the *REW* 3683b; Dauzat, s.v. *gord*, from ON *garð-r* 'fence, wall'.

88. Norm. *guiseau* 'type of eel' in the patois of the Seine basin, may be from ON *°visla* 'weasel', according to Barbier, *RLR*, LIII (1910), 40. The etymology is not entirely satisfactory, because we would expect *°vile* from *°visla*, since Fr. *île* is from an older [izla]; moreover [v-] is to be expected in coastal Normandy for ON [w-].

89. *guitan* 'gadus luscus' in the patois of Côtes-du-Nord, Ille-et-Vilaine, may be from ON *hviting-r* 'type of whale', but perhaps used of smaller fishes, as Swed. *vitling*, Dan. *hvilling* 'whiting' which are related to the ON word (Hellquist, s.v.

vitling). The ON etymology is suggested by Barbier, *RLR*, LXVII (1935), 321.

90. Norm. *ha, har, haus, haû, haut*, ONorm. *hal* 'dog-fish' are from ON *há-r*, s.m. 'dog-fish'. According to Barbier, *RLR*, LXVII (1935), 323–4, the ON form gave two original forms in the Romance of Normandy: *har*, which went on to lose its final consonant in some areas, and *hal*, from which the plurals *haout, hau* and *haut* were formed. Barbier gives an example from 1531, and Sjögren, p. 401 cites an example from 1694 in Philippe Falle's *History of Jersey*. Cotgrave lists the word as *hal*. The Norman word is unusual in that it seems to come from the ON nominative singular *há-r* with the flexional ending retained; this is the only such example in ON words in Normandy. Also unusual is Dutch *haai* 'dog-fish' which looks like the ON dative, although Falk-Torp, s.v. *Haa* II state that Dutch *haai* renders the ON pronunciation of *hár* which had a nasal vowel. OF *haye* 'dog-fish' is from Dutch, rather than directly from Norse (Valkhoff, s.v. *haye* 'requin').

91. Norm. *have*, s.f. in the patois of Jersey 'filet à crevettes avec manche' in the *Glossaire du patois jersiais* seems to be from ON *háf-r* 'net'. Cf. *havenet*, §92.

92. *havenet, haveneau*, s.m. 'shrimping-net' is from ON *háf-net*, cf. ON *háf-r* 'net' and ON *net* 'net' and Shetland Norn *avnet* 'small net'. The fact that both ON words meant 'net' may be explained by an original meaning of 'small net with which the fish are taken out of a net' (Jakobsen, *Etymological Dictionary of the Norn Language*, s.v. *avnet*). Norm. *havenet* is the original form whereas *haveneau* shows a change in suffix when -*net* was no longer a meaningful element. Other changes of suffix are obvious in Norm. *havelet*, French Brittany *haveneau, haveleau*, Breton *avenel*, Anjou, Blaisois and Berry *aveneau* and Poitou *avagneau*. Cf. also Valognes *ravenet* with [r-] for [h-] (Duméril). Barbier, *Miscellanea Lexicographica*, XXV (1944), 57, was not aware of the fact that in ON *háf-r*, *r* was the flexional ending; he expresses skepticism as to whether the element -*net* in *havenet* really is the ON word 'net', and thought that ON *háf-r* gave an ONorm. °*havre* of which *havenet* was a diminutive. The fact is that *havenet* was the original Norman

form, and the forms in -*el* and -*eau* arose when -*et* was thought to be a suffix. The ON etymology of *havenet* is also in Bloch, Dauzat and the *DG*.

93. Fr. *homard*, Norm., ONorm. *houmar*, OF *hommar* (1547, *DG*, but first attested in 1532 according to Bloch) from ON *humar-r* 'lobster', a West Norse form (Hellquist, s.v. *hummer*). The -*d* is due to analogy with Fr. words in -*ard*. Dauzat's statement that Fr. *homard* is from Dan. *hummer* and the statement in the *REW* 4236 that it is from Swed. *hummer*, are misleading and make the reader believe the Fr. word is a recent loan. Cf. Fr. *homarderie*, s.f. 'lobster-ground'.

94. Norm. *houblin, houlin, houvet, houvelin, houvlin*, s.m. 'edible crab' is from ON *hóf-r* 'hoof' and by extension 'claw' according to Barbier, *Miscellanea Lexicographica*, XXV (1944), 59.

95. *lingue*, s.f. (Littré), s.m. (*DG*) 'ling' may be of ON origin (cf. OIcel. *lyng-fisk-r* 'ling-fish') rather than from Eng. *ling*, the etymology in the *DG*, Dauzat and the *REW* 5065. The word was first attested in the 14th c. as *leynge*. The possibility of ON origin was suggested by A. Thomas, *Essais de philologie française*, p. 329.

96. Fr. *lieu*, s.m. 'pollack', Guernsey *lü* is probably of ON origin, cf. OIcel. *lý-r* 'pollack' (*REW* 5193) from an earlier °*liuhi-z* (Holthausen, *Vergleichendes und Etymologisches Wörterbuch des Altwestnordischen*, s.v. *lȳ-r*); thus Fr. *lieu* must be from an ODan. °*liu-ʀ*, with stress on the first element of the diphthong, all unstressed vowels becoming [ə] in Normandy. Guernsey *lü* seems to be a local development after the original form became monosyllabic. For the Romance treatment of ODan. [iu], cf. below §114 and §125.

97. *marsouin*, s.m. 'porpoise', first attested at Dieppe in 1396 as *massouyn, marsouyn* (Bloch) is from ON *marsvin* 'sea-hog, kind of whale' (*REW* 5378; Bloch, Valkhoff, s.v. *marsouin*). Cf. also *marsouin arrière* 'sternson', *marsouin avant* 'stemson' from the nautical use of *marsouin* as 'forecastle awning'.

98. Norm. *orfi*, s.m. 'bécasse de mer' (Bessin, Jersey), *horfi* (Jersey), *olfi* (Granville), ONorm. *horfilz*, s.m. pl. (in Gouberville's *Journal*, Poppe, p. 40) is probably from ON *horn-*

fisk-r 'garfish', according to Joret, *Romania*, IX (1880), 125. German *Hornfisch*, proposed by Alessio, I, 201, is itself taken from the Low German dialects of the coast; cf. Barbier, *RLR*, LXVII (1935), 309. For the change [fisk] to [-fi], cf. *Figard* which was *Fiscgardum* in ONorm. documents (*REW* 3683b, Longnon, p. 284).

99.   *raguet*, s.m. 'nom d'une petite morue verte' (Trévoux, 1771); *raquet*, s.m. '. . . rebut de la pèche des morues qui consiste en petites émules. . . .' (*DG*, 1832) are connected by Barbier, *RLR*, LXV (1927), 29 ff. with Icel. *rask* 'fish refuse', Norw. *rask* 'fish waste', Swed. dial. *rask* 'rubbish, trifle' and ODan. *rask* 'trifle'. *Raquet* is then the diminutive of an ONorm. °*raske* 'rebut', from which are derived Norm. *râquillon* 'rebut' and Fr. *racaille*, s.f. 'rebut de la société', attested as *rascaille* in the 12th c. with possible influence of *canaille*. Cf. Norm. *raquillon*, s.m. 'trognon de poire ou de pomme' in Valognes (Duméril) and 'rebut de foin que mangent les bestiaux' in Cherbourg; cf. also Norm. *raquilloner* (patois of Percy, M.) 'faucher dans les herbages'.

100.   *rogue*, s.f. 'salted cod's roe' with the primary meaning 'fish-eggs', first attested in 1723 (*DG*) seems to be from ODan. °*rogn* (cf. OIcel. *hrogn* 'roe'). The ON etymology is in Bloch and Sjögren, p. 392; Dauzat and the *REW* 7363 give the impression that *rogue* is a recent loan from Danish or Norwegian, and Kluge, s.v. *Rogen* states that Fr. *rogue* was borrowed from Danish in the 18th c. However the word is widespread in Normandy; in addition to *rogue*, the form *roque* is found in the Bessin, with the adjective *rocu* 'couvé', also *rogu* 'laitu' in La Hague, *rogué* 'poisson femelle qui n'a pas encore frayé' in the Pays de Bray. The form *rogē* 'louse egg' is used in the Seine Inférieure (*ALF*, Map 757) and must be related. With this wide use in Normandy, the word must be older than the 18th c.

101.   Fr. *rohart*, ONorm. *rohal, rohart, rouart, roal,* s.m. LL *rohallum* 'ivoire de morse et d'hippopotame' (*Larousse*) are probably from ODan. °*rosswal-r* (cf. OIcel. *hross-hval-r* 'walruss'). The etymology is in Bugge, *Romania*, III (1874), 157 and in the *REW* 4215. For the ONorm. forms, cf. Delboulle, *Romania*, XXXIV (1908), 614 and *Coutumiers de Normandie*,

ed. Tardif, I, 115. Cf. also *Romania,* LXXI (1950), 132. The
Irish forms *rosualt, rosuall,* cited by Marstrander, p. 107 are
also of ON origin. ONorm. *galerous, galerox* 'walruss' which
the *REW* 9495; Joret, *Romania,* XI (1882), 618; and A. Thomas,
Romania, XL (1911), 618 ff. derive from Norse offers difficulty
because Dan. *hvalros* is not a native Norse word, but a loan
from Dutch (Falk-Torp, s.v. *hvalros*).

Animals and Birds

102. ONorm. *bequerel,* s.m. 'agneau qui vient d'avoir un an'
(Godefroy) may be from ON *bekri* 'ram' + a Fr. suffix. Godefroy gives an example from 1397: ". . . lesquelles betes appellees
bequereaulx audit pays de Caux. . . ."

103. Norm. *crax* (Guernsey), s.m. 'traquet, petit oiseau
brun' may be from ON *krák-r,* s.m. 'crow, raven'. Norm. *crax*
is listed by Métivier.

104. *duvet,* s.m. 'down', OF *dum* (12th c.), Norm. *dum,*
dun (Jersey, Guernsey), Norm. *dœm* (Bessin) are from ON
dún-n 'down'. The word is common in the Norman patois: Norm.
dumet, deumet 'duvet', cf. OF *dumet*; Norm. *dumer, deumer*
'muer'; Norm. *édumer* 'élaguer'; *édeumer* 'enlever les petites
branches qui poussent le long du tronc'. Fr. *duvet,* attested since
1310 may be the result of the Breton change of [m] to [v].
Among the forms with [v] are: *duveté,* adj. 'couvert de duvet'
(Cotgrave, 1611); MFr. *duvée,* s.f. 'duvet'; *duveteux,* adj. 'qui
a beaucoup de duvet', since the 16th c.; MFr. *enduvetter* 'cou-
vrir de duvet' (Cf. *FEW,* III, 180). The *FEW* explains the form
dumet as due to an incorrect back-formation from the simple
form *dum* with influence of *plume.* Cf. also Bloch, Dauzat, s.v.
duvet and the *REW* 2797. Eng. *down* is also from ON *dún-n*
(*OED,* s.v. *down,* sb.).

105. OF *edre,* s.m. 'plume d'eider, édredon' attested from
the 13th to 16th c. seems to be from ON *æðr,* s.f. 'eiderduck'.
The form *edre* seems to indicate that the word does not go
back to 900; we should have then expected a form *erre; Fr.

frère was at the stage *fradre* ca. 900. The word was reborrowed later as *eider* (cf. §299).

106. Norm. *harousse,* s.f. 'haridelle, vieux cheval usé, mauvaise jument' is from ON *hross,* s.n. 'horse, mare'. The ON etymon retained [hr-] which had already simplified to [r-] in the bulk of the ODan. words in Normandy. An anaptyctic vowel was introduced in Normandy, where [hr-] was an unfamiliar group. Bloch, s.v. *haridelle,* states that OF *harace* appears with the translation *equus spadix* 'cheval bai' which agrees with ON *hárr* 'gray-haired', and thus may be of ON origin. Cf. also Sjögren, p. 395.

107. OF *hele,* s.m. 'elk' is from ON *elg-r,* s.m. 'elk'. Cf. Nyrop, *Romania,* XXXV (1906), 563.

108. Norm. *héri,* s.m. 'male hare', which Duméril traced to ON *heri* 'hare', has been studied by Barbier, *Miscellanea Lexicographica,* V (1929), 202. Barbier has shown that Duméril's etymology is phonetically impossible, since we should have expected a form *here from ON *heri.* Perhaps Norm. *héri* is from an older *héril (from ON *heri* contaminated with OF *connil*).

109. ONorm. *mave, mauve;* Norm. *maûve* (patois of Guernsey) s.f. 'sea-gull' may be from ON *má-r,* pl. *mávar,* s.m. 'sea-mew' rather than of Eng. origin as proposed by Bloch, s.v. *mouette.*

110. *Ouville,* S.-I., earlier *Ulfeville,* may contain ON *ulf-r* 'wolf' (cf. *Louvetot,* attested earlier as *Lupitot*). The name was discussed by Jakobsen, *Danske Studier,* 1911, p. 68. J. A. des Gautries, p. 234 and pp. 460–2 has shown that the place-name may be of Frankish origin, however.

111. Norm. *ridet,* s.m. 'lièvre mâle' (Orne, Bas-Maine, ALF Map 769) may be related to ON *riða* 'to cover (speaking of copulation of horses)'. Barbier, *Miscellanea Lexicographica,* V (1929) 202 mentions a similar construction in Dutch *rijder* 'connin mâle' from *rijden* 'to ride, used of the male animal in copulation'. Barbier rejects an ON source because ON [-ð-] would not normally give Fr. [-d-], but cf. §7. The word *ridet* appears only in Normandy, a fact which would make ON origin probable.

112. Norm. *sandon*, s.m. 'sandworm' (*Transactions of the Guernsey Society*, VI (1906), 530) may be from an ON *sandorm-r* from ON *sand-r* 'sand' and *orm-r* 'snake' but perhaps in Primitive Norse 'worm' as in English, and in German *Wurm*.

113. Norm. *vico, vidco*, ONorm. *widecos* (Marie de France, *Fable* 24), *vitecotz* in Sire de Gouberville's *Journal* (Moisy, Glossaire, s.v. *vico*), s.m. 'woodcock' may be from an ON *við-kok-r* (*við-r* 'wood', *kok-r* 'cock'). Littré's etymology, Eng. *woodcock* does not explain the use of the word in the Cotentin (cf. *ALF* Map 121). The word is also found in the Channel Islands (Métivier, s.v. *vidco*), and in the place-name *Videco(s)ville* near Valognes (Métivier).

Other Words Pertaining to Animals

114. Fr. *bréchet*, OF *brichet, bruchet*, Norm. *brûquet, briquet, bréquet*, s.m. 'breast-bone, carina (of fowl)' may be from an ODan. *briūsk* (cf. OIcel. *brjósk*, s.n. 'cartilage'). The original ONorm. form must have been *briesk* + suffix. Thus *briesket* underwent simplification of the diphthong, giving the various forms with [e], [i] and [y]. Bloch, s.v. *bréchet* and the *FEW*, I, 536b give Eng. *brisket* as the source, but Eng. *brisket* is not attested until a century later than the Fr. word. The wide use of the word in Normandy, Anjou, Poitou, Maine and Vendôme would seem to exclude the English source and make a Norse source likely.

115. Norm. *falle*, s.f. "jabot des oiseaux, gorge, estomac', also MF *fale* (Normandy, 16th c.) has been traced by the *FEW*, III, 392 to ON *fal-r*, s.m. 'socket of a spear-head into which the shaft fits' with a semantic shift in Normandy similar to that of Lat. *canna* in Italian. Among the derived forms are: Norm. *fallu* 'qui a du jabot, qui fait l'important'; Norm. *falue*, s.f. 'galette très lourde'; Norm. *défaller*, v.r. 'découvrir la gorge', Canadian *éfaler* 'découvrir la gorge', Norm. *falle-rouge* 'rouge-gorge'. For a complete discussion of the word, see the *FEW*, III, 392. The ON etymology is also given by

the *REW, Nachträge,* 6957; Dauzat, s.v. *fale* and *Français moderne,* V (1937), 142.

116. Fr. *flèche,* OF *fliche,* since 1195; Norm.-Pic. *flique,* s.f. 'flitch of bacon', Norm. *flique* 'morceau de pain, de viande; flocon de neige'< ON *flikki,* s.n. 'flitch of bacon'. The vowel in Fr. *flèche* (cf. OF *fliche*) has been explained as due to crossing with OPic. *flec* of West Germanic origin. Cf. *FEW,* III, 621; Bloch, Dauzat, s.v. *flèche* and the *DG* s.v. *flèche* 2.

117. AN, Pic. *floc,* Norm. *flo, flio* 'troupeau', Jersey *floquet* 'foule' seems to be from ON *flokk-r,* s.m. 'body of men, band, troop' rather than from AS *floc* (*FEW,* III, 844a).

118. Norm. *horn,* s.f. 'head' (Héloup, Alençon Ouest, O., *ALF Supplément,* I, 270b) may be the same word as Norm. *heune* 'head' (from ON *hún-n*). ON *horn,* s.n. 'horn (of cattle)' is perhaps too far semantically from Norm. *horn* 'head'.

119. OF *timbre,* s.f. 'peau de martre, d'hermine' (Godefroy), s.m. in Littré; Moisy, *Glossaire,* gives *timbre,* s.m. 'un certain nombre de peaux de martre'. Sjögren, 403–4 derives the word from ON *timbr,* gen. *timbrs,* s.n. 'a set of forty skins'. For the change in gender, Sjögren sees influence of Fr. *nombre.* However, Falk-Torp, s.v. *tømmer,* state that the meaning 'number of skins' came to Norse from German; this raises the question of whether the ON word had that meaning in 900.

120. OF *titre, tistre, tristre,* s.m. 'relais où sont postés les chiens' has been traced to ON *treysta* 'to make strong, rely on, dare, venture' (Dauzat. s.v. *titre* 1; *REW* 8884; A. Thomas, *Romania,* XXIX (1900), 202). Gamillscheg 846a derives the Fr. word from Eng. *tryst,* but the latter is from ON *traust* (*OED,* s.v. *tryst;* cf. ME *traisten* 'to trust' from ON *treysta*). The ON etymology of Fr. *tristre* is not completely satisfactory phonetically and semantically.

Designations of Persons

121. Norm. *bruman,* s.m. 'nouveau marié, fiancé le jour de son mariage' is probably from ODan. *°brūðman,* cf. OIcel. *brúð-maðr,* s.m. 'bridegroom's man, bridesman', perhaps also

'bridegroom' (*FEW*, I, 559b). The Norman word seems to have been attested as a common noun in 1521, but already in 1198 it appears in the Rolls of the Norman Exchequer as the surname of three different persons; cf. *Romania*, LXX (1949), 127.

122. Norm. *brun, bru*, ONorm. *bru* 'nouvelle mariée', Norm. *kužbrun* 'demoiselle d'honneur dans un mariage' appear to be formed from *bruman* (cf. §121), hence the nasal vowels in some of the forms (*FEW*, I, 559a). However, it seems quite likely, as the *FEW* states, that ON *brúð-r*, s.f. 'bride' was introduced into Normandy in the 10th c. Norm. *bru* 'nouvelle mariée' may then be a different word from Fr. *bru* 'daughter-in-law', a much earlier Germanic loan. Cf. the quotation from Fabri in the *DG*, s.v. *bruman*, dated 1521: "Nous disons la bru et le brumen, au lieu de fiancée et fiancé".

123. AN *daie*, s.f. 'servante' may be from ON *deigja*, s.f. 'servant-maid, dairy-maid', rather than from ME *deye* which is itself of ON origin (Hellquist, s.v. *deja*). The *FEW*, III, 63a traces AN *daie* to ME *deye*.

124. ONorm. *escipre, eskipre*, OF *eschipre*, s.m. 'matelot' is from ON *skipari*, s.m. 'seaman', according to Falk, p. 5; Nyrop, *Wörter und Sachen*, VII (1921), 97; and Hopfgarten, p. 24. The word was used during the 12th and 13th c. (Godefroy, III, 392a).

125. ONorm. *esterman(t), est(i)reman, estirman*, s.m. 'pilote, timonier, matelot' may be from an ODan. *°stiūrimann* (cf. OIcel. *stýrimaðr* 'skipper, captain'). Cf. AS *stéoresmann* of ON origin (Falk-Torp, s.v. *Styrmand*). The ODan. word is attested in runic inscriptions as *styrimanns* (Skautrup, I, 163). A number of synonymous words, *esturmen, estrumen*, etc. may be of West Germanic origin (Valkhoff, s.v. *esturman*). Cf. also Falk, p. 5, n. 2. There was probably an original ONorm. *°estiereman* (cf. ONorm. *estiere* 'rudder') in which the diphthong was reduced to either [e] or [i].

126. *Fermanville, Farmanvilla* in the 12th c. may contain the ON surname *farmaðr*, gen. *farmanns*, originally s.m. 'seaman'. However, J. A. des Gautries, p. 446 has shown that the

name may be either Scandinavian or Frankish. Cf. also L. Musset, *Études germaniques*, II (1947), 136ff.

127. *Flottemanville* (M.) the name of two localities in the Cotentin, one of which is in the Bocage and the other in La Hague, comes from ON, cf. OIcel. *flottamað-r*, gen. *flottamanns*, ODan. °*flottamann*, s.m. 'one who flees'. Cf. L. Musset, *Études germaniques*, II (1947), 136. Cf. also *Flotmanby* in the East Riding of Yorkshire, where Scandinavian settlement was intense.

128. *Godeman*, a Norman surname may be from ON, cf. OIcel. *góð-r* 'good' and ODan. °*mann-r* (OIcel. *mað-r*, gen. *manns*) 'man'. Cf. L. Musset, *Études germaniques*, II (1947), 141.

129. *gouine*, s.f. 'femme de mauvaise vie' was according to Mignard pronounced with initial [k] (cited by G. Adams, *Words and Descriptive Terms for Woman and Girl in French and Provençal and Border Dialects*, p. 36) and according to Littré, is from ON *kvinna*, s.f. 'woman'. The change from initial [k] to [g] may be due to the fact that the word passed from Normandy to Brittany, where such a change was quite normal in certain contexts. Thus, the masculine formation *gouin* 'matelot d'une mauvaise tenue', which Littré says is the *masculin burlesque* of *gouine*, was first attested in the 15th century in the following phrase: *Ne se pouvoient aider ne tourner leurs chevaulx, tellement estoient goins.*

It is striking that a number of words beginning with the element *guen-* are disparaging names for women. It might be suggested that *gouine* became *guen-* whenever a suffix was added to the original monosyllabic form. In many dictionaries, the meaning 'woman' is given as a secondary meaning, but historically this may not have been true. Cf. the following words which may be derived from *gouine*, and which are all of the feminine gender: *guenille* 'tattered garment, old rag, trollop'; *guenillon* 'piece of rag, slut, slattern'; *guenipe*, s.f. 'trollop, drab, strumpet'; *guenon* 'she-monkey, ugly woman'; *guenuche* 'ugly woman'; OF *gueniche, guenichon* 'petite guenon' (16th c., *DG*); ONorm. *guenette* 'femme de mauvaise vie' (D. Ferrand, V, 113); ONorm. *gouines* 'sales femmes'; ONorm. *gouyne* 'femme de mauvaise vie, coquine'; Norm. *guenette* 'femme de

mauvaises moeurs'; Norm. *guenipe* 'vilaine femme'. Cotgrave
also lists *guenonnée* 'a most beastlie wench. . . .' It is quite
possible that 'woman' is the primary meaning of our word, and
that such meanings as 'rag' and 'monkey' are later develop-
ments. Gamillscheg 495b and *REW* 4724 give reconstructed
ON forms *°gnipan* and *°knipa* to explain *guenipe*, without considering the large number of words with different suffixes
which must be related. However, Meyer-Lübke was aware that
the word belonged to western France, and saw the possibility
of ON origin because of the word's geographical extension.

130.   ONorm. personal name *Guesmanus, Wesman, Wes-
manus* in 11th century texts is from ON *vest-mað-r*, gen. *vest-
manns*, s.m. 'a man from the west, from the British Isles, especially Ireland', according to L. Musset, *Études germaniques*, II
(1947), 134.

131.   Fr. *guilledou* in *courir le guilledou* 'to frequent night
haunts', OF *guildrou* in the 16th and 17th centuries is of western
French origin and quite probably from ON *kveldulf-r* literally
'evening wolf' attested as a nickname in *Egil's Saga*, and used
in Iceland of the fretful mood caused by evening, according
to Cleasby-Vigfusson, s.v. *kveldulf-r*. This etymology for Fr.
guilledou is not a doubtful construction as Meyer-Lübke states
in the *REW* 3935. Originally proposed by S. Bugge, *Romania*,
III (1874), 151, the ON etymology is also given by Dauzat,
s.v. *guilledou*, and Alessio, I, 168. It is to be noted that the
modern form *guilledou* is closer to the ON source as far as
the last syllable is concerned; the [r] of OF *guildrou* is non-
etymological.

132.   ONorm. personal name *Guineman*, also *Vineman*<
ODan. *°Vinnu-mann* (cf. OIcel. *vinnu-maðr* 'laborer, man-servant
on a farm'). The ON etymology was suggested by L. Musset,
Études germaniques, II (1947), 133.

133.   Norm. *gyèn* (Guernsey) 'bande, troupe' in the *ALF
Supplément* I, 18b, Locality No. 399 may be from ON *gang-r*
'gang', or it may have been the Eng. *gang* which was recorded.

134.   Norm. *herquette*, s.f. 'rateau' (patois of Vire, listed
by Du Bois and Duméril) may be related to ON *herkja* 'to drag

oneself along'. Cf. also Norm. *herque*, s.f. 'dégingandée' (patois of Rouen, in D. Ferrand, V, 118).

135. Norm. *hore, horette*, s.f. 'jeune fille' is from ON *hóra*, s.f. 'harlot' (*REW* 4177, Sjögren, pp. 381–2). A derived form seems to be OF *horier, hourier* 'man who frequents prostitutes'; if OF *horier* is related to Norm. *hore*, ON *hóra* was certainly introduced to Normandy with the meaning of the ON word. Godefroy, IV, 486–7 gives a number of variants: *holier, houlier, hurier* and others, some of which may be of West Germanic origin, since the word is attested for Malmédy, Luxemburg and the Moselle as well as for Normandy. Cf. George C. S. Adams, *Words and Descriptive Terms for Woman and Girl in French and Provençal and Border Dialects*, p. 39.

136. Fr. *matelot*, OF *matenot*, s.m. 'sailor', Guernsey *matnot* 'companion' is from ON *mǫtunaut-r* 'mess-mate' according to Bugge, *Romania*, III (1874), 156; Falk-Torp, s.v. *Matros*; Kluge, *Seemannssprache* & *Et. Wb.* s.v. *Matrose*; Dauzat; *Histoire de la langue française*, p. 187; Falk, p. 8 and Gamillscheg 599a. A Dutch etymology is given by Hellquist, s.v. *matros*; Bloch, Dauzat, *DG*, Valkhoff, s.v. *matelot* and *REW* 5405. An extensive discussion of the word is given by Nyrop, *Wörter und Sachen*, VII (1921), 82–96, in which he favors the Dutch etymology; semantically the older meaning of *matelot*, 'homme attaché à un autre et partageant avec lui son hamac' is closer to Middle Dutch *mattenot* 'compagnon de couche' than to ON *mǫtunaut-r*; however the Dutch word appears a century later than the Fr. word (Valkhoff). When it is considered that Dutch *matroos* was borrowed from French (Van Wijk-Franck s.v. *matroos*), it may well be that Dutch *mattenot* received its meaning, at least, from French. The ON form cannot be rejected on phonetic grounds since the ODan. form was probably **matunaut-r*; at any rate words with *ǫ* in Old Icelandic are regularly treated as words with *a* in French, English and Irish.

137. The ONorm. personal name *Sokeman* may be from ON *sókn*, s.f. 'attack, prosecution, parish' (L. Musset, *Études germaniques*, II (1947), 139). Cf. also the title *Lacman* (from ON *lǫgmaðr*) 'magistrate, lawman' probably taken to be a personal name in Normandy (J. A. des Gautries, p. 69, n. 12).

138.   ONorm., AN *utlague, uslague, hutlage, uilage,* s.m. 'outlaw' may have come directly from ON *útlagi,* s.m. 'outlaw' rather than from AS *útlaga,* which is itself of ON origin (*OED,* s.v. *outlaw,* sb.), The appearance of the word in Benoît's *Chronique des ducs de Normandie* (Valkhoff, Moisy), a work which was written in Touraine (Pope, p. 500) would certainly seem to exclude the English word.

139.   *Walmannus, Waumannus* (LL of Normandy) 'whale-fisher' was used until the 12th century in the northern Cotentin and the Dive as a common noun. The same root is found in the ONorm. family name *Le Vauman,* and in *Le Gaument,* which still exists. Cf. L. Musset, *Études germaniques,* II (1947), 137; and also *Romania,* LV (1929), 585. The words are probably from ON **hvalmann-r* 'whale-fisher'.

Parts of the Body

140.   Fr. *brichet,* s.m. 'poitrine, estomac, devant de l'estomac' 1596–1759 (*FEW,* I, 537a); Paris *bréchet* 'estomac'; Norman *bruchet* 'creux de l'estomac' is an extended use of Fr. *brichet, bréchet* 'os saillant de la poitrine d'un animal'. See above, §114.

141.   Norman *fale,* s.f. 'gorge des hommes' is an extension of Norman *fale* 'jabot des oiseaux'. See above, §115.

141b.   Norm. *horn* (patois of Héloup, Alençon Ouest) 'head'. See above, §118.

142.   Norm. *heune,* s.f. 'head' is an extended use of *hune* 'top (of the mast)'. See above, §40.

143.   Norm. *lippe,* s.f. 'lip', a word frequently used by David Ferrand (see ed. A. Héron, V, 128) < ODan. *lippe* 'lip'; according to Hellquist, s.v. *läpp,* it is a native Scandinavian word, judging by its extension in the dialects. In the map in Dauzat's *Les Patois,* p. 98, it can be seen that *lippe* is almost exclusively Norman; the area where *lippe* is used is separated from the area where *lèp* is used, the latter in the north-eastern corner of France, by words of the *babine* type, which cut across Picardy and the Pas de Calais.

144. ONorm. *mague*, s.f. 'stomach' (patois of Rouen) in the works of David Ferrand (cf. ed. A. Héron, V, 131) is very probably from ON, cf. OIcel. *magi*, s.m. 'stomach, belly'. Cf. also *magus*, adj. m. pl. 'pansus' in David Ferrand.

145. Fr. *quenotte*, s.f. 'tooth', OF *quenne, cane* 'tooth' is from ON *kinn*, s.f. 'cheek' according to the *DG*, Dauzat, s.v. *quenotte*; the *REW* 4702, and Pope, p. 14, who gives OF *cane* in the sense of 'jaw'. The *FEW*, II, 689, derives *quenotte* from a Frankish °*kinni* because of the wide extension of the word in France; a Frankish form better explains such forms as *rechigner* because of the palatalization. OF *kenne* 'cheek' cited by Bloch, s.v. *quenotte* is semantically very close to the ON word, but Bloch prefers the Frankish source. Fr. *quenotte* was first attested in 1642 in Oudin (*DG*).

Terrain

145a. Norman *acre*, s.f. and m., LL of Normandy *acra* 'acre', OF *acreé* 'étendue d'une acre de terre' (*FEW*, I, 23a) was first attested in the Latinized form in a text from Laval (Mayenne) in 1125 (Bloch, s.v. *acre* and *FEW*, I, 23a). The word still survives in Normandy in the Eure, Pays de Bray and the Vallée de Yères. W. von Wartburg and Bloch believe that the English word *acre* was brought to the continent after 1066. The *DG*, p. 19 gives an ON etymology, although ON *ákr* is attested in the meaning of 'field' rather than as a measure of the field. A third possibility, that of continental Saxon origin, is suggested in *Normannia*, V (1932), 398. Moisy, *Dictionnaire*, s.v. *acre* thought that the Norman word was brought to England after 1066. Although the oldest attested Scandinavian forms of *ákr* do not designate a measurement, an example in *Christian V's Danske Lov* seems to refer to the concept of measurement rather than to the field itself: the *Ordbog over det Danske Sprog*, I, 354, s.v. *ager* gives the meaning in this example as 'en af de lige store dele, hvori en ejendoms pløjede jord indeles. . . .' Discussing the semantic development of the same word, Skautrup, I, 62 states: "*Ager* betyder måske oprindelig 'græsningsmark', men i Danmark blev det betegnelsen for den mindste jordenhed, som dyrkedes". With historical and geographical factors taken into consideration, and in view of the fact that Norman *acre* is the normal phonetic outcome of ON *ákr*, Scandinavian origin is probably more likely than English origin, although pre-viking Saxon origin cannot be overlooked.

146. ONorm. *aye* 'isle' is from ON *ey*, s.f. 'island' (*FEW*, III, 337b). The word also seems to survive in the names *Jersey*, *Guernsey*, *Aurigny* and *Chausey*.

146a. The Norm. place-name *Bactot*, C. may contain ON *bakki*, s.m. 'ridge, bank of a river' (J. A. des Gautries, p. 32).

147. Norm. *bec*, LL of Normandy *beccus*, s.m. 'brook' in place-names (*Bolbec, Clarbec*, etc.) is from ON *bekk-r* 'beck, brook' (*FEW*, I, 208a).

148. Norm. *-bye* in the place-names *Hambye, Houguebye* seems to be from ON *bý-r* 'farmhouse, farm, town'.

149. Norm. *-clive* in *Verclives*, E. and ONorm. *Wite Clive*, name of a rock near Evreux mentioned in 1224 is from ON *klif*, s.n. 'cliff' (*FEW*, II, 780a; Longnon, p. 286).

150. *crique*, s.f. 'creek, cove, small bay'< ON *kriki*, s.m. 'bay' (Sjögren, p. 389; *REW* 4776; Bloch, *DG*, s.v. *crique*). The word also appeared as ONorm. *crigue* in 1336 (*la crigue de Vateville*), cited by L. Delisle, *Etude sur la condition de la classe agricole en Normandie au moyen-âge*, p. 291. (*DG*)

151. Norman *dale* in place-names< ON *dal-r*, gen. *dals*, s.m. 'dale, valley' in the following names: *Les Dales* (Pays de Caux), *La Dale* (hamlet in the Evrecin), *Becdal, Verdal, Bruquedalle, Croixdalle, Dieppedalle, Oudale, Sensedalle*, etc. (Joret, *Des caractères et de l'extension du patois normand*, pp. 35–36). The use of the word with the article shows that it must have survived for a time as a common noun in Normandy.

152. Norman *delle*, s.f.; *dellage*, s.m. Moisy defines *delle* as 'groupe de pièces de terre en labour, compris dans ce que l'on appelle un *dellage*, c'est-à-dire dans la région d'une plaine en labour où les pièces ont leurs sillons tracés dans le même sens et aboutissent le plus souvent à un chemin d'exploitation commun'. Moisy adds, that the word *delle* always carries a particular (proper) name; *delle de l'Ormelée, delle de la Cavée*,

etc. The word appeared in Latin documents of Normandy as *dela* (1216). Moisy, *Glossaire*, s.v. *delle*. It may be from ON, cf. OIcel. *deild*, s.f. 'dole, share'.

153. Norman *dis* in the Channel Islands place-name *Les Terres du Dis*< ON, cf. OIcel. *dys*, gen. *dysjar*, s.f. 'cairn' (Kendrick, *Archeology of the Channel Islands*, I, 132). Kendrick also derives *Déhus* from ON *dys* which is phonetically difficult (*A History of the Vikings*, p. 219, n. 1); the second syllable of this Guernsey place-name appears to be ON *hús*, 'house' which also occurs in continental Norman names.

154. Norman *écore* s.f. 'berge escarpée' (Moisy, *Glossaire*). The word is perhaps from ON *skor*, pl. *skorar* 'rift in a rock or precipice'. There is also a *Rue des Écores* at Trouville.

155. *Écrehou*, name of a small rock near Jersey, formerly *Escrehou*< ON *°sker-holmr*, from ON, cf. OIcel. *sker*, gen. pl. *skerja* 'rock in the sea, skerry', s.n. and ON, cf. OIcel. *hólm-r*, gen. *hólms*, s.m. 'islet'. This etymology is found in J. Jakobsen, *Danske Studier* (1911), p. 62.

156. *Étainhus* (S.-I.), formerly *Estainhus*< ONorw. *steinhús*, s.n. 'stone house'. The first element ON, cf. OIcel. *stein-n*, gen. *steins*, s.m. 'stone' also occurs in *Étaintot* (S.-I.) which was formerly *Estaintot*.

157. *Hague* in the Norman place-names *Le Hague-Dike* seems to be ON, cf. OIcel. *haka*, gen. *hǫku*, s.f. 'chin' but also used to denote a promontory in Danish and Norwegian toponymy. Cf. Michel de Bouard, *Annales de Normandie*, III (1953), 7, who has shown that [g] would not have survived in this word if the word was older than the Viking invasion. Similarly *dike* (< ON *díki*) would have given *°di* if it were a Germanic word of the 6th or 7th centuries.

158. Norm. *hogue, hougue*, s.f., *houguet, houguillon*, s.m. 'hill' is from ODan. *°hǫug-r*, cf. OIcel. *haug-r*, s.m. 'hill' (Sjögren, p. 391). The word is common in Norm. place-names, and appears as *Hoga, Hogua* in 1040; cf. J. A. des Gautries, *Annales de Normandie*, III (1953), 27. Cf. ME *hogh* 'hill' of ON origin (Björkman, p. 69). Cf. also the *ALF Supplément*, I, 145a for Guernsey *hūg* 'petite colline'.

159. Norm. *houmet*, s.m. 'presqu'île, pâturage assis sur l'eau' in the patois of Guernsey (cf. Métivier) is a diminutive of ONorm. °*houme* from ON *hólmi*, s.m. 'islet'. The same ON form gave Norm. -*homme* in *Engehomme, Robéhomme, Le Homme* (Longnon, p. 286). Cf. the form *Holmus* in 1027, later *Le Homme*, now *L'Isle Marie*, M., J. A. des Gautries, *Annales de Normandie*, I (1951), 27. There was another ON form *hólm-r* which must have become ONorm. °*hol*, then -*hou* in such names as *Quettehou*, and *Le Hou*, an islet near Guernsey. Cf. also the form *Torhulm* (J. A. des Gautries, p. 423).

160.   ONorm. *houle*, s.f. 'cavité où retirent les poissons au bord de la rivière', Norm. *houlette*, s.f. 'trou de lapin', Norm. *houlet*, s.m. 'brèche, ouverture', Fr. *houle*, s.f. 'swell, surge (of sea)' seem to be from ON *hol*, s.n. 'hollow, cavity' or ON *hola*, s.f. 'hole, hollow'. Cf. Bloch, s.v. *houle*. Pic. *haule* 'port' must be a different word; cf. Norm. *hable* 'port' §64.

161.   The Norm. place-names *Houlgate, Houlbec* seem to contain ON *hol-r*, adj. 'hollow'. The second element of *Houlgate* may be ON *gata* 'way'. Cf. F. Stenton, *Transactions of the Royal Historical Society*, 4th ser., XXVII (1945), 5.

162.   The Norm. place-name *La Londe* is from ON *lund-r*, s.m. 'grove' (Longnon, p. 287). Cf. also *Achelunda* in the 11th c. and *Catelun*, gen. *Catelunti*, now *Catelon* (J. A. des Gautries, pp. 375, 403).

163.   Norm. -*mare* in place-names seems to be from ON *mar-r*, s.m. 'sea'. The word may have been a feminine noun in Normandy originally (cf. the forms *Longuemare, Rondemare*, Longnon, pp. 287–8). The retention of [a] in -*mare* shows that the word does not go back to earlier Germanic invasions; moreover forms in -*mare* do not appear outside of Normandy. There is reason to believe that Fr. *mare*, s.f. 'pool, pond', which may be the same word as Norm. -*mare*, is also from ON *mar-r* 'sea'. Fr. *mare* is first attested in Marie de France (*DG*, s.v. *mare*).

164.   Norm. *mer*, ONorm. *merc*, Norm. *merque* 'marque, borne' seems to be from ON *merki*, s.n. 'boundary, mark'. ON *merkja*, v. tr. 'to mark' may be the source of ONorm. *merker* 'to mark' (12th–16th c.), OF *merchier* and Fr. *marquer*. Bloch,

s.v. *marquer*, attributes the vowel of that word to influence of *marcher* 'presser' and influence of Ital. *marcare*. However, the alternation of [ar] and [er] was sufficiently frequent in Normandy and in Paris to account for the form *marquer* without influence of other words, but the possibility of contamination cannot be overlooked. In the same family are Fr. *amers*, s.m. pl. 'tous les points d'une côte visibles de la mer qui peuvent servir d'indication pour diriger les navires' and Fr. *amarque* 'balisse, bouée' attested in 1678 (*DG*).

165. Norm. *mielle*, s.f. 'terre sablonneuse près de la mer' has been traced to ON **mjelar*, s.m. pl., cf. OIcel. *mel-r*, s.m. 'sand-bank, gravel-bank', appearing also in England as *miol* (Sjögren, p. 396). The word survives as a common noun in *Jersey, Guernsey, Cherbourg, La Hague*, M. and *Percy*, M. The etymology OIcel. *mel-r* given by the *REW* 5486 is impossible for reasons of phonetic chronology. Norm. *mielle* is found in the plural in place-names, and was wrongly used as a masculine by Victor Hugo in *Les Travailleurs de la mer* when he wrote *au Grand-Mielles*.

166. Norm. *tangue, tanque*, LL of Normandy *tangua, tanga* (12th c.) 'slimy sea sand used as fertilizer' seems to be from ON *tangi*, s.m. 'point projecting into the sea' contaminated with ON *þang*, s.n. 'seaweed'. Sjögren, p. 392 gives ON *þang* as the source, but Barbier, *Miscellanea Lexicographica*, XX (1939), 99, rejects the latter word stating that *tangue* means 'sea-sand' particularly 'sea-sand mixed with ooze', and that there is nowhere to be found any connection of *tangue* with seaweed. Cf. Norm. *tangon* 'sea-weed' < ON, cf. OIcel. *þang* 'sea-weed'. It seems that the confusion in the two words is due to the fact that both are used for fertilizer in Normandy. See also above, §52, and below, §196. The ON etymology is also given by Hellquist, s.v. *tang* 1, Falk-Torp, s.v. *Tang* II; cf. also English *tangle* which is ultimately from ON *þang* (*OED*, s.v. *tangle*, sb. 1).

167. Norman *torp, tourp* in place-names < ON, cf. OIcel. *þorp*, s.n. 'isolated farm, thorp, village; open, unsheltered place'. The use of the article indicates that the word must have

survived for a time as a common noun: *Le Torp* (M., S.-I.), *Le Tourp* (M.). Cf. Longnon, p. 288.

168.   Norman *-tot* in place-names< ON *toft*, cf. OIcel. *topt* [toft], s.f. 'homestead, a place marked out for a house, the mere walls or foundation of a former building'; the word appeared in the LL of Normandy as *toftum*, according to Bengt Holmberg, *Tomt och Toft som appellativ och ortnamselement*, p. 139; cf. also pp. 138–140 and pp. 236–265 for a listing of the Norman localities with the element *-tot*. Cf. also Longnon, pp. 290–291.

169.   Norman *tuit, thuit*, in place-names is from ON, cf. OIcel. *þveit*, s.f. 'a clearing of land' in ON place-names. In Normandy, the word must have survived as a common noun, as the form *Le Thuit* (E.) shows. It exists in a number of compounds: *Bliquetuit, Brennetuit* (S.-I.), *Écriquetuit* (E.), *Long-Thuit, Le Milthuit, Vauthuit* (S.-I.) and also followed by proper names such as *Thuit-Hébert*. Cf. Eng. *-thwaite* in place-names of ON origin.

170.   Norm. [ur] (patois of Guernsey) 'coteau en pente stérile' may be from ON *urð*, s.f. 'a heap of stone fallen from a hill'. The word is in the *ALF Supplément*, I, 145a, s.v. *montagne*.

Houses and Structures

171.   ONorm. *boel(e)* 'cour, masure' may be from ON *ból*, s.n. 'farm'. The *FEW*, I, 594b derives our word from a Germanic **budil*, stating that an ON form with l-suffix is not attested, without mentioning ON *ból*.

172.   Norm. *-bu* in *Tournebu, Bourguébus* and *Carquebut* seems to be from ON *bú*, s.n. 'household' (*FEW*, I, 580b, Longnon, p. 283).

173.   *Butot*, S.-I. is from ON *búðartopt* 'terrain where booth is built', from ON *búð*, s.f. 'booth' according to J. A. des Gautries, p. 43.

174.   Norm. *bur*, s.m. 'habitation', Norm. *buron* 'petite cabane' are from ON *búr*, s.n. 'woman's apartment, pantry,

storehouse' according to the *FEW* I, 630a. Fr. *bure*, s.f. 'blind shaft' is of West Germanic origin.

175. Norm. *cotin*, s.m. 'maisonette'; *cotie*, s.f. 'rangée de maisons'; Norm. *-cot(t)e* in place-names, are from ON *kot*, s.n. 'cottage, small farm, hut'. Cf. J. A. des Gautries, *Études germaniques*, VIII (1953), 1–5.

176. *Ecalles*, S.-I. (cf. *Ecclesia de Scalis*, 13th c.) is from ON *skáli*, s.m. 'hut, shed' (A. Vincent, *Toponymie de la France*, p. 161).

177. Norm. *-gard* in place-names (*Auppegard, Bigards*) is from ON *garð-r*, s.m. 'fence, wall, yard' (Longnon, p. 284). If *Bigards* is related to OIcel. *bý* 'bee' as Longnon suggests, then perhaps ONorm. *bigre* 'garde forestier chargé de chercher les essaims d'abeilles dans les forêts et de les mettre dans les ruches', attested since 1418 is from an ON *°bíkari*, rather than from a Frankish *°bíkari* as stated in the *FEW*, I, 360a. The fact that ONorm. *bigre* was limited to Normandy is an argument in favor of ON origin.

178. *La Guerche*, the name of several localities in Brittany, Maine, Anjou, Poitou, Touraine, Marche and Berry, also *La Guierche*; *Wirchia*, ca. 1120; *Guircia*, ca. 1036 is probably from ON, cf. OIcel. *virki*, s.n. 'stronghold, castle'; cf. *Castrum Wirchiae* in 1077. For the change from [ir] to [ier], cf. *vierge< virge* and *cierge< cirge*. The word has been studied in detail by Fritz Askeberg, *Namn och Bygd*, XXXII (1944–1945), 176–203. Guy Souillet, *Mémoires de la société d'histoire et d'archéologie de Bretagne*, XXIV (1944), 25–46, believes that the word is of Frankish origin, which is not very likely in view of the geographical distribution of the place-name in question.

179. Fr. *hangar*, s.m. 'shed' may be from ODan. *°hems-garð-r* cf. OIcel. *heimis-garð-r*, gen. *-garðs*, s.m. pl. 'homestead'. Gamillscheg, 506b proposed a Middle Dutch *°ham-gaerd*, which Valkhoff rejects because *ham* in Dutch does not mean 'house' but 'lopin de terre. . . .' The LL forms *hangardum* and *hangardium* in 15th century texts, cited by Littré, s.v. *hangar* bear a close resemblance to the ON word. At Thaon (C.) the local form is *hākor* (Guerlin de Guer, *Le Parler populaire de la commune de Thaon*, p. 40).

180. Norman -*hus* in *Étainhus* < ON, cf. OIcel. *hús* 'house'; Longnon, p. 286, and Pope, p. 90.

181. Norman *stal* in *Danestal* (C.), *Darnestallum* in 1198; *Darnestal* (C.) and *Danetal* (S.-I.) may be from ON *stall-r*, gen. *stalls*, s.m. 'crib, manger'. The retention of [s] may be a pronunciation influenced by spelling.

182. *Surrain* (C.), *Surrehain* in the 11th century: *Surreheim* in the 12th century; *Surayn* in 1417 seems to contain ON, cf. OIcel. *heim-r*, gen. *heims*, s.m. 'a place of abode' or ON, cf. OIcel. *heima*, adv. 'home' (A. Vincent, p. 160). The Old Saxon *hêm* suggested by A. Vincent as an alternate etymology would not have given the diphthong, and, moreover, the Saxon word appears in Normandy as -*ham*: *Ouistreham, Étreham, Le Ham* (Longnon, p. 182).

Plants, Trees and Related Words

183. *Bouquelon* (E.) seems to contain ON, cf. OIcel. *bók*, gen. *bókar* 'beech'.

184. *Bruquedalle* (S.-I.) may contain ON, cf. OIcel. *brúk*, s.n. 'a heap, esp. of seaweed'.

185. *Bû-sur-Rouvres* was attested in 1373 as *Le Busc* and is derived by A. Vincent, p. 160, from Old Norse (cf. Swedish *buske* 'bush'). However, it is not likely that the Scandinavian word, which is incidentally not attested in the older stages of the Scandinavian languages (cf. Hellquist, s.v. *buske*) existed with a long vowel. Pope, p. 22, derives this Norman place-name from ON *bú*, but this does not account for the old form *Le Busc*. The form -*busc* still occurs in *Alvimbusc, Elvimbusc*, etc. (S.-I.). The problem is not solved, especially when we consider that *busc* alternates with *bosc* in ONorm. texts. Cf. P. Lechanteur, "Bosc et bois dans les noms de lieux de la Normandie," *Annales de Normandie*, II (1952), 70.

186. Norman *coque* (patois of Pont-Audemer) 'petite veillotte'; Norman *coq* (patois of Yères) 'veillotte de foin, de trèfle'; Norman *coqueron* (patois of Bray and Yères); *coquet* (patois of Louviers) 'veillotte de foin' < ON, cf. OIcel. *kǫkk-r*,

dat. *kekki*, s.m. 'lump'. The *FEW*, II, 826a derives the words from English, but according to Falk-Torp, s.v. *Kok*, English *cock* 'haystack' is also of ON origin. Cf. AN *coketer*, MFr. *cocheter* 'mettre en petits tas'.

187. Norman *dogue*, s.f. (patois of Yères, Bray, Tôtes, Bayeux, Thaon, Bissières, C.; Le Havre, Pont-Audemer); Norman *doque*, s.f. (patois of Bessin, La Hague, Jersey, Guernsey, Deux-Jumeaux, C.); Norman *doche*, s.f. (patois of Bayeux); OF *doque*, s.f. 'patience (name of a plant)' < ON *dokka*; cf. Swedish *ådokka* 'Seerose' *FEW*, III, 111b, Valkhoff, s.v. *doque*. The word was first attested in 1314 in the *Chirurgie* of Henri de Mondeville. W. von Wartburg believes that the same word in other parts of northern France is of West Germanic origin, but his suggestion of English influence on the continent is hard to accept.

188. *Ecquetot* (E.), *Ectot* (S.-I., M.), older *Esketot* seems to contain an ON, cf. OIcel. *eski* 'ash grove' according to F. Stenton, *Transactions of the Royal Historical Society*, 4th series, XXVII (1945), 5. Longnon, p. 291, thought it was from ON *eiki* 'oak'.

189. Norman *étoc*, s.m. 'tronc d'arbre', ONorm. *étoc* in the *Journal du Sire de Gouberville* (cf. Moisy, *Glossaire*, s.v. *étoc*) may be ON, cf. OIcel. *stokk-r*, gen. *stokks*, s.m. 'stock, trunk, block, log of wood'.

190. Norman *Étoublon* (M.) (cf. above, §162) may contain the ON word *stofn*, gen. *stofns* (but *stofu-* in compound words), s.m. 'stump of a cut tree'. The final element is ON *lund-r* 'grove'.

191. ONorm. *giernote* 'terrenoix' (attested first in 1220); Norman *gênotte* (patois of Bayeux, Val de Saire, Argentan, La Hague, Vire, Jersey), s.f. 'terrenoix'; Norman *gernotte* (Le Havre) 'avoine à chapelet' < ON *jarð-hnot* 'earth-nut' from *jorð*, gen. *jarðar*, s.f. 'earth' and ON, cf. OIcel. *hnot*, s.f. 'nut'. Cf. Swed. *jordnöt*. The etymology is found in the *FEW*, III, 236a, and A. Thomas, *Romania*, XXIX (1900), 177. Valkhoff, s.v. *giernote* also cites an ONorm. *jarnotte* in 1793. Cf. S.-I. [jèrnòt] *ALF Supplément*, I, 218 ab. Cf. Norm. *égernotter* 'ramasser des tubercules de la gernotte', and *gernotier*, s.m.

'ramasseur des tubercules de la gernotte', both attested for Le Havre.

192.   Norman *hague*, s.f. 'fruit de l'aubépine' (patois of the northern Cotentin, Joret, *Mélanges de phonétique normande*, s.v. *hague*; patois of Valognes, Duméril, s.v. *hague;* patois of Jersey, *Glossaire du patois jersiais*, s.v. *hagues*); ONorm. *hague* in the *Journal du Sire de Gouberville* (Moisy, *Glossaire*, s.v. *hague*)< ON **hag*, cf. OIcel. *hag-þorn*, s.m. 'hawthorn'.

193.   Norman *han*, s.m. (patois of La Hague, Créances, Briqueville, M.) 'souchet à longues racines, cyperus longus'< ON, cf. OIcel. *hampr*, s.m. 'hemp'. A diminutive form is Norman *hanette* (patois of Briqueville, M.) listed by F. Lechanteur, *Annales de Normandie*, I (1951), 133. Cf. also Charles Joret, *Mélanges de phonétique normande*, pp. 29–30.

194.   Norman *haveron*, s.m. 'wild oats' (Moisy, *Glossaire*; Duméril, Cotgrave) may be ON, cf. OIcel. *hafri* 'oats' contaminated with OF *avenon* (< *avena*). The aspirate [h] indicates Germanic influence; the *DG* derives *haveron* from [Old] High German *habaro*. Cf. English *haver* 'oats' of ON origin.

195.   Norman *Limbeuf* (E.) and *Lindebeuf* (S.-I.) have as their first element ON, cf. OIcel. *lind*, s.f. 'lime-tree' (Longnon, pp. 281–282).

195a.   *Seltot* (S.-I.) may contain ON *selja*, s.f. 'willow'; Gautries, p. 55.

196.   Norman *tangon*, s.m. (patois of Jersey, Guernsey) 'une espèce de varech'< ON, cf. OIcel. *þang*, s.n. 'sea-weed' Cf. Sjögren, 392–393; Barbier, *Miscellanea Lexicographica*, XX (1939), 99. See also above, §52 and §166.

197.   Norman *tondre*, s.m. 'amadou' (patois of Val de Saire, La Hague, Jersey, Guernsey and Pays de Bray)< ON, cf. OIcel. *tundr*, gen. *tundrs*, s.n. 'tinder'. The first known example of the word is in the *Bestiaire de Philippe de Thaon* (Sjögren, p. 402). The word has also been treated by Dauzat, s.v. *tondre*; *REW* 8984; Hellquist, s.v. *tunder*; Duméril, and Moisy, *Glossaire*, s.v. *tondre*. Cf. Norm. *tondroier* 'boîte à amadou'.

198.   Norman *torve*, s.f. 'gazon combustible, tourbe' (patois of Guernsey) may be ON, cf. OIcel. *torf*, s.n. 'turf, sod' or ON,

cf. OIcel. *torfa*, s.f. 'turf, slice of sod'. The word is listed by Métivier and by Moisy, *Glossaire*, s.v. *torve*.

199. Norman *Tournebut* (M.) and *Tournetot* (E.) seem to have as first element ON, cf. OIcel. *þorn*, gen. *þorns* 'thorn' (Longnon, pp. 283 and 291).

200. Norman *vamôque* 'poppy' < ON *°valmoge*, cf. OSwed. *valmoghe* 'poppy'; the etymology is in Barbier, *Zeitschrift für französische Sprache und Literatur*, LIII (1929–1930), 7; this is cited by the *REW*, 9134a, which also mentions Norm. *avamōk*.

201. Norman *vandine* 'laminaria saccharina' may be connected with ON, cf. OIcel. *vinda* 'to wind'. Cf. Barbier, *ZFSL*, LIII (1929–1930), 18.

202. *varech*, s.m. 'sea-weed'. Cf. §70.

203. Norman *vélingue* 'laminaria saccharina' is from ON *°vringla* (according to the *REW* 9576a, cf. Norw. *vringle* 'to wind') but now listed with a less concrete meaning of 'to cavil, prevaricate'. Barbier says that this etymology originally proposed by Behrens is semantically sound, but that we should expect *°vérangle* or *°véringue*. Cf. Barbier, *ZFSL*, LIII (1929–1930), 18. We have found another plant-name *verlingue* 'cowry' used at Guernsey in the *Transactions of the Guernsey Society of Natural Science and Local Research*, VI (1906), 530. There seems to be no reason why the change from [r] to [l] could not have taken place in *vélingue*. Barbier prefers a Frankish source, however.

Implements, Clothing, etc.

204. OF *bague*, s.f. 'baggage' may be from ON, cf. OIcel. *baggi*, s.m. 'pack, bundle' (Dauzat, s.v. *bagage*, Kluge, s.v. *Bagage*). The *FEW*, I, 204, however, states that the word is widespread in French dialects, and derives it from *°baga*. Cf. also the *DG*, s.v. *bagues*, s.f. pl., first attested in 1421; *bagage* was first attested in the 14th century (*DG*, s.v. *bagage*).

205. Fr. *baratte*, s.f. 'churn', OF *barate*, s.f. 'ruse, confusion, agitation' may be from ON, cf. OIcel. *barátta*, s.f. 'contest, fighting, battle' (Dauzat, Battisti-Alessio, s.v. *baratta*, *REW*

943a). The word must have undergone a semantic change from 'fighting' to 'confusion, mixture' to 'instrument for churning'. The *REW* 943a gives OF *barater* 'to deceive' as a derived form, as well as Fr. *baratter* 'to churn'. In the same family are OF *barat*, s.m. 'ruse', OF *barateau*, s.m. 'petite baratte'; *baratement*, s.m. 'fraude, tromperie'; OF *barateor*, s.m. and adj. 'trompeur'; *barateressement*, adv. 'frauduleusement'; OF *baraterie*, s.f. 'tromperie'; OF *barateus* adj. 'trompeur'. OF *barat*, s.m. survives in the patois of Guernsey with the meaning of 'fraude, fraudeur' (Métivier, s.v. *barat*). Cf. also Fr. *barattage*, s.m. 'churning', *baratton*, s.m. 'plunger, dasher (of churn)', and Fr. argot *baratin*, s.m. 'big talk'.

206.   ONorm. *barde*, s.f. 'hache du charpentier' (patois of Rouen) used by David Ferrand, ed. A. Héron, V, 15; ONorm. *bardage*, s.m. 'l'éclat de bois détaché par l'outil du charpentier de la pièce qu'il façonne'. The word may be from ON, cf. OIcel. *barða*, s.f. 'kind of axe'.

207.   Norman *bédière*, s.f. 'mauvais lit' (patois of Pays de Bray, Yères, Le Havre), Norman *bédière* (patois of Pont l'Evêque) 'lit'; a derived form is Norman *bédo* 'dernier-né d'une couvée' (patois of the Bessin, Thaon), Norman *bdo* (patois of Val de Saire), Norman *bdot* (patois of La Hague), Norman *bédot* (patois of Manche), and Norman *bedasson, bedanson* (*FEW*, I, 311b). ONorm. *bédière*, s.f. 'lit de valet d'écurie' occurs in David Ferrand (Rouen, 17th century); cf. Moisy, *Glossaire*, s.v. *bédière*. These words are probably from ON, cf. OIcel. *beð-r*, gen. *beðjar*, s.m. 'bolster, bedding, bed', but which may have also meant 'animal's litter'; Falk-Torp, s.v. *Bed* I state that the basic meaning 'animal's litter' is found in Norwegian dialectal *bed* as well as in OSwed. *bædhil*. W. von Wartburg's English etymology is difficult to accept for a word so widespread in Normandy, with even a related form *bedouque* attested as far south as the Island of Elle, Vendée. A similar word of West Germanic origin is found in the Walloon area (*FEW*, I, 311b). Cf. above, §7 for retention of [-d-].

208.   ONorm. *bele*, s.m. 'manteau garni de fourrures' in Wace's *Roman de Rou* may be derived from ON, cf. OIcel.

belg-r, gen. *belgs*, s.m. 'skin of a quadruped taken off whole'. The word is listed in Moisy's *Glossaire*.

209. Norman *bingue*, s.f. 'panier rond en osier à deux anses' (patois of Jersey) in the *Glossaire du patois jersiais* may be from ON, cf. OIcel. *bing-r*, s.m. 'bed, bolster' but perhaps also 'bin, receptacle of some sort'; cf. Danish *bing* 'grosse Kiste, Kasten, Kornkiste', Swedish dialectal *bing* 'Korn- oder Mehlkiste', Norwegian *binge* 'bin' (Falk-Torp, s.v. *bing*).

The word *bin à muš* 'ruche' attested for Jort, C. and Ponts, Avranches, M., *ALF* Map No. 1174 (Localities 345 and 368) may contain the same ON word; in those localities 'hive' is literally 'bin for bees' with *mouche* instead of *abeille* (Cf. Gilliéron, *L'Abeille, passim*).

210. Norman *bra*, s.f. 'poix des cordonniers' (patois of Jersey), listed in the *Glossaire du patois jersiais* may be derived from ON, cf. OIcel. *bráð*, s.n. 'pitch'. Cf. above, §11 for Fr. *brai* 'tar'.

211. Norman *brie* (no gender given) 'instrument pour pétrir la pâte' (Moisy, *Glossaire*, s.v. *brier* 'pétrir'); the word may be from ON, cf. OIcel. *bryðja*, s.f. 'a sort of trough'. However, the related verb *brier* has some relation to Fr. *broyer*, OF *breier* 'to pound, crush, mill' of West Germanic origin (Cf. *DG*, s.v. *broyer*).

212. Fr. *canif*, s.m. 'knife', first attested in the diminutive form *canivet* in a 12th century Norman work (*DG*, s.v. *canivet*) may be from ON, cf. OIcel. *kníf-r*, gen. *knifs*, s.m. 'knife' (*DG*, s.v. *canif*). Dauzat, s.v. *canif* believes that the word is of English origin; however, the English word *knife* is itself of ON origin (cf. *OED*, s.v. *knife*). According to the *FEW*, II, 802b, 803a, the geographical extension of the word in French makes the ON origin unacceptable; the *FEW*, like the *REW* 4723 and Bloch, s.v. *canif* traces the word to Frankish.

213. Norman *cliu* (patois of Jersey) 'petit morceau d'étoffe'; OF *clut* 'morceau'; ONorm. *clustrel* with non-etymological *s* 'haillon'; OF *clutel* (14th century); OF *cluter* 'mettre en morceaux, estropier'; OF *clutet* 'langes' (13th century) < ON, cf. OIcel. *klútr*, gen. *klúts*, s.m. 'kerchief', *FEW*, II, 801b. OF

recluter 'rapiécer' may have been contaminated with *recruter* (Auguste Scheler, s.v. *recruter*).

214. Fr. *croc*, s.m. 'hook', first attested in the 12th century in an Anglo-Norman work (*DG*, s.v. *croc*) is from ON, cf. OIcel. *krókr*, gen. *króks*, s.m. 'hook' according to Dauzat, s.v. *croc*, *REW* 4780, and Alessio, I, 305; cf. Eng. *crook* < ON *krókr* (*OED*, s.v. *crook*). Bloch states that *croc* is of Frankish origin, while the *FEW*, II, 1359a implies that the element *krokk* is onomatopoeic.

215. Norman *drāg* 'grande botte pour marcher dans l'eau' (patois of Bessin); Norman *dragye* 'marcher dans l'eau' (patois of Bessin); Picard *draguelle* 'espèce de grande chausse à l'usage des pêcheurs', also *driguelle* are from ON, cf. OIcel. *drag*, s.n. 'iron rim under the keel of a boat or a, sledge' according to the *FEW*, II, 152a. This is semantically difficult; it might be suggested that ON *draga* 'to drag' entered the Norman patois as *draguer* 'to drag'; hence *dragye* 'to walk in the water, i.e., with difficulty, by dragging the feet'; the noun *drāg* 'botte' would then be derived from the verb.

216. *élingue*, s.f. 'cordage à noeud coulant', OF *eslinge* 'fronde' (12th century), identified as a Norman and Picard word (cf. Bloch, s.v. *élingue*) is probably from ON, cf. OIcel. *slyngva*, 'to sling' integrated into the Romance of Neustria as *eslinguer*. The etymology from Old Norse is in Gamillscheg 347a; cf. English *sling* which has its meaning from Norse (Falk-Torp, s.v. *slynge*). It is difficult to understand why Bloch and Dauzat, s.v. *élingue*, derive the word from English. Cf. also Fr. *élinguer*, v. tr. 'to sling, raise by a sling'.

217. OF *esclot*, Norman *ecllo* (patois of Guernsey) 'trace du pied d'un cheval' (Métivier, s.v. *ecllo*) is probably from ON, cf. OIcel. *slóð*, s.f. 'track, trail'. The ON origin of French *esclot* is in the *OED*, s.v. *slot*, sb. 3; cf. also Falk-Torp, s.v. *sløi*, where it is stated that English *sleuth-hound*, Middle English *sloth*, *sleuth* 'track' are of ON origin.

218. ONorm. *escreppe*, s.f. 'besace' (Moisy, *Glossaire*) may be from ON, cf. OIcel. *skreppa*, s.f. 'scrip, bag'. However, Holthausen, *Etymologisches Wörterbuch des Altwestnordischen*, s.v. *skreppa*, derives the OIcel. word from OF *escreppe*. Hol-

thausen, in the *Etymologisches Wörterbuch der englischen Sprache*, p. 174, derives English *scrip* from Latin *scirpea*. Hellquist, s.v. *skräppa* 'ränsel' 3, cites OSwed. *skræppa*, Danish dialectal *skræppe* as well as the OIcel. form *skreppa*, tracing these words to various Germanic roots. The existence of the word in a modern Danish dialect would be a valid argument to preclude borrowing of the OIcel. form from French.

219. Norman *flouette*, s.f. 'girouette' (patois of Cherbourg, St-Sauveur, Val de Saire), Norman *flouet* 'girouette' (patois of La Hague), as well as Fr. *flouette*, s.f. 'girouette d'un vaisseau' 1643 may be from ON, cf. OIcel. *flug*, s.n. 'flight' or ON, cf. OIcel. *fluga*, s.f. 'fly' (*FEW*, III, 642b).

220. Norman *gloe*, s.f. 'log' may be from ON, cf. OIcel. *glóð*, s.f. 'red-hot embers' with a transfer in meaning. The word is listed by Moisy, *Glossaire*.

221. *girouette*, s.f. 'weather-vane', Norman *virouette* (patois of Jersey) in the *Glossaire du patois jersiais*; ONorm. *wirewite, wirewire* and *wenute* (which probably should be read *°werwite*), according to A. Thomas, *Essais de philologie française*, p. 401< ON, cf. OIcel. *veðr-viti*, s.m. 'vane' (Dauzat, *REW* 9516, Falk-Torp, s.v. *vede*; Falk, p. 42; Frahm, p. 62; Bloch, s.v. *girouette*). The ONorm. word appears to have been contaminated with *virer* while Fr. *girouette* for a more normal *°guirouette* must have undergone the influence of *girer* or been influenced by the spelling. Another spelling is OF *gyrouet*.

222. Fr. *guichet*, s.m. 'wicket-gate', Norman *viquet* 'petite porte' (patois of Jersey) in the *Glossaire du patois jersiais*; OF *wiket* seem to be derived from ON, cf. OIcel. *víkja* 'to move, turn' (*OED*, s.v. *wicket*) or ON, cf. OIcel. *vík* 'hiding place' (Bloch, s.v. *guichet*, states that the 12th century meaning of the Fr. word was that of ON *vík*, cf. OF *guischer*, v.i. 'glisser vivement comme une anguille qui s'échappe des mains de celui qui la tient' which may be from ON *víkja*). The ON etymology is given by Bloch, Dauzat, the *DG*, s.v. *guichet*; cf. the *OED*, s.v. *wicket*. At Thaon, C,. the word appears as *gyiše* 'guichet de tonneau' (Guerlin de Guer, *Le Parler populaire de la commune de Thaon*, p. 305). However, F. Lechanteur, *Annales de Normandie*, I (1951), 105, states that Norman *viqué* 'petite

porte ménagée dans les tonneaux' tends to disappear, both as far as the word and the object it represents are concerned as the line of non-palatalization of [k] is crossed.

Fr. *guichetier*, s.m. 'turnkey' (since Cotgrave, 1611) *DG*.

223. Fr. *harnais*, s.m. 'harness', OF *herneis, harnois*, s.m: 'armure, équipage d'un homme d'armes' first attested in the *Couronnement de Louis* in the 12th century (*DG*) < ON °*hernest* 'army provisions' reconstructed after OIcel. *vegnest* 'provisions for traveling'; the etymology is given by Bloch, Dauzat, s.v. *harnais*; Alessio, I, 58 and 328, *REW* 4119. The OF meaning survives in certain expressions, such as *suer dans son harnois* 'être mal à l'aise sous ses vêtements', *blanchir sous le harnois* 'vieillir dans le métier des armes', *endosser le harnois* 'embrasser la profession des armes' (*DG*). Extended meanings are found in Fr. *harnais de pêche* 'fishing-tackle', and Norm. *hernais* 'charrette à deux roues avec ressorts' (Jersey). Cf. the form *rarné* in the Eure (*ALF*, Map 684). Among the derivatives are: OF *harneschier*, 1200, Fr. *harnacher* 'to harness'; *harnachement*, s.m. 'harnessing, 1561; *harnacherie*, s.f. 'harness-making'; *harnacheur*, s.m. 'harness-maker', 1402; *déharnacher* 'to unsaddle', 12th c.; *déharnachement*, s.m. 'unsaddling', 1636; *enharnacher*, v. tr. 'to harness', 13th c.; *enharnachement*, s.m. 'harnessing'.

224. Norm. *herquette*, s.f. 'rake'. Cf. §134.

225. OF *huve*, s.f. 'sorte de coiffure, de bonnet', OF *huvet*, s.m. 'bonnet de femme'; OF *huvette*, s.f. 'bonnet' may be from ON *húfa*, s.f. 'cap, bonnet'. Cf. §39.

226. Fr. *loure*, s.f. 'bagpipe; slow dance in ¾ or 6/4 time'; Norm. *loure* 'type of flute, flageolet, bagpipe'; Fr. *lourette* 'petite musette'; MFr. *lourer* 'jouer de la loure'; Norm. *lourer* 'jouer de la musette, jouer de la flûte'; Fr. *loureur* 'celui qui joue de la musette'; Norm. *lourer* 'pleurnicher'; *loureur* 'pleurard', probably from ON *lúðr*, ODan. *lūr* 'trumpet' (Cf. Dauzat, s.v. *loure*) but since ON [ū] would have given Norm. [y], some other force must have been at work to account for the form *loure*, such as contamination from Lat. *lura* 'pipe, hose', as suggested by the *FEW*, V, 465a. Cf. Eng. *lowdrer* from ON *lúðr* (Hellquist, s.v. *lur*, 1).

227.   ONorm. *rêquet*, s.m. (patois of Rouen, 17th c.) 'gaule',
ONorm. *rêquer* 'abattre les fruits' may be from ON *reka* 'to
push violently'. For the Norman words, cf. D. Ferrand, V, 190.

228.   ONorm. *sairch* 'shirt' may be from ON, cf. OIcel.
serk-r, pl. *serkir* 'shirt'; the word occurs in the fabliau *La Veuve*;
cf. Gunnar Tilander, *Romania*, LII (1926), 478.

229.   OF *tangre, tangue*, s.m. 'tang of a knife'< ON, cf.
OIcel. *tangi*, s.m. 'the pointed end by which the blade is driven
into the handle'. Godefroy defines *tangre* as 'extrémité du cou-
teau qui est dans le manche'. Cf. above. §52.

230.   OF *tierre*, s.m. and f. 'corde ou chaîne fixée par un
anneau à un pieu pour attacher les chevaux ou les vaches' (Godefroy); ONorm. *tière* 'tether' in the *Journal du Sire de Gouberville*, (E. Poppe, p. 64); *Norman tière* (patois of Coutances,
Val de Saire, Percy, M., Bayeux, Pays de Caux) 'chaîne pour
attacher les chevaux, etc.'; Norman *tière* 'the stake to which
the animals are attached' (patois of Lisieux); cf. L. Hédin,
Annales de Normandie, I (1951), 68. The word is undoubtedly
from ON, cf. OIcel. *tjóðr*, dat. *tjóðri* 'tether'; the ODan. form
tioðr had a diphthong stressed on the first element and was
equated with OF words with the diphthong [ie]. Cf. A. Thomas,
Romania, XXIX (1900), 177–178, and *Mélanges d'étymologie
française*, p. 108. English *tether* is also of OF origin (*OED*,
s.v. *tether*, sb.).

231.   Fr. *tille*, s.f. 'hachette de couvreur'<ON, cf. OIcel.
telgja, v. tr. 'to cut', also s.f. 'person who cuts' Norm. [tiy]
(patois of Thaon) 'outil de charpentier' (Guerlin de Guer, *Le
Parler populaire de la commune de Thaon*, p. 389). The word
is discussed by Dauzat, s.v. *tille*, *REW* 8621; Joret, *Romania*,
IX (1880), 435, and the *DG*, s.v. *tille* 2.

232.   Norm. *tro*, s.m. 'pétrin' (patois of Jersey, *Glossaire
du patois jersiais*; patois of Fresville, Montebourg, M. and Sainte-
Geneviève, Quettehou, M.; patois of Sark and Jersey; *ALF*, Map
No. 1006, Localities No. 386, 393, 397, 398), ONorm. *trou*,
s.m. 'huche' (Moisy, *Glossaire*, s.v. *trou*) in a Norman document of 1333. The word must be from ON, cf. OIcel. *trog*, s.n.
'trough'.

233. *vadrouille*, s.f. 'tampon de laine fixé au bout d'un bâton pour nettoyer le pont' (*DG*) first attested in 1690 may be from ON *váð*, s.f. 'stuff, cloth' with an expressive suffix *-ouille*. OF *vadel*, a naval term meaning 'handle, stick, swab' may be the same root. *Vadrouille* is also used in Normandy as 'torchon mouillé que les boulangers avant d'enfourner mettent au bout d'un bâton et promènent sur les parois du four. . . .', also 'toile grossière servant pour les emballages' cited by P. Barbier *ZFSL*, LIII (1930), 1–4. Furthermore, the use of *vadrouille* in the sense of 'prostitute' seems to have originated in Norman ports; for the semantic change, cf. *guenille* and *guenipe*, also meaning 'rag' and 'strumpet'. For semantic, phonetic and geographical reasons, the word seems to be a Scandinavian word integrated into the Romance of Neustria in the tenth century.

Miscellaneous Adjectives

233b. *Blactot, Blacquetuit*, Norman place-names, may contain ON *blakki* 'dark brown', as does Eng. *Blacktoft* (J. A. des Gautries, pp. 175–6).

234. OF *blestreus*, adj. 'couvert de boutons, de tumeurs'; OF *blestre* 'tumeur'< ON, cf. OIcel. *blæstri*, dative of *blástr*, s.m. 'swelling of the body or a limb' (*FEW*, I, 416a).

235. Norman *brague*, adj. 'vif, qui fait du bruit'< ON, cf. OIcel. *braka* 'to creak, crack', according to Storm, *Romania*, V (1876), 172; it is of Celtic origin according to the *FEW*, I, 478b ff.

236. Norman *Caudebec, Caudecote* has as its first element ON, cf. OIcel. *kaldr*, neuter *kalt*, adj. 'cold'; cf. J. A. des Gautries, *Études germaniques*, VIII (1953), 1 ff.

237. Norman *écomant*, adj. 'dégoûtant, affadissant', AN *escomos, escoymous*< ON, cf. OIcel. *skǫmm*, s.f. 'shame' through an unattested Norman *°écomer*. The etymology is given by Barbier, *RDR*, IV (1912), 123; A. Thomas, *Romania*, XXXIX (1910), 221; cf. also *Romania*, XXXIX (1910), pp. 88 and 90.

238. AN *ein* 'own' in the expressions *de son eine talent* and *de ayndegré* 'de son propre gré' is derived by the *FEW*, I, 55b, from an Anglo-Saxon *°eign* (sic). However, the Anglo-Saxon form was *āgen*. The vowel indicates borrowing from ON, cf. OIcel. *eiginn* 'own' which may have been integrated in the Romance of Neustria on the continent before 1066, or from the Scandinavian languages still surviving in England after 1066 into Anglo-Norman through Middle English.

239. *guingois*, adj. 'skew' first attested in the 15th century in a Norman work seems to be of the same family as OIcel. *vingla* 'to confound', *vinglaðr* 'confused' and *vingl* 'disturbance, vacancy of mind'; cf. Fr. *esprit de guingois*. The ON etymology is given by the *REW* 9547.

240. OF *guiscart, guiscard, guicart*, adj. 'rusé, astucieux, avisé' (Godefroy) is according to the *REW* 9558 from ON, cf. OIcel. *wiskr* 'scharfsinnig'; with -*ard* suffix; cf. also ON *hvískr*, s.n. 'whisper'. Godefroy, s.v. *guiscart*, states that *guichard* is still used in Normandy in the sense of 'rusé, astucieux'. OIcel. *wiskr* (i.e. *visk-r*) is not listed in the dictionaries. Cf. Huguet, s.v. *guiscard* ". . . qui en la langue des Normands signifie ingénieux et rusé," in a work of 1616.

241. ONorm. *ignel, isnel*, Norman *inel* 'vif, ardent', first attested in Wace's *Roman de Brut* (cf. Moisy, *Glossaire*, s.v. *inel*) is, in the opinion of Ernst G. Wahlgren, *Studia neophilologica*, III (1930–1931), 116–129, from ON *°sniell*; Wahlgren states that a West Germanic *snel* neither explains the initial [i] nor the alternation of [sn] and [gn] as does the ON form, which could easily explain the development of the prothetic vowel to the stage [i] and also the palatalization of the interior consonantal group. Cf. also *Romania*, LVII (1931), 595. The OIcel. form was *snjall-r* 'swift'.

242. *joli*, adj. 'pretty' has been derived from ON *jól*, s.n. pl. 'a great midwinter feast in heathen times' by the *REW* 4590; Falk-Torp, s.v. *Jul*; Alessio, I, 300; Bloch and the *DG*, s.v. *joli*. Dauzat, following Brøndal, expresses some skepticism, and the *OED*, s.v. *jolly*, states that Fr. *joli* is of uncertain origin. The ON etymology offers semantic difficulties. The word appeared in the 12th century as *jolif*.

243. *rogue,* adj. 'arrogant' < ON, cf. OIcel. *hrókr* 'arrogant'; cf. Dauzat, Bloch, s.v. *rogue,* adj., and the *REW* 4213. Cf. OF *se roguer,* v. refl. 'faire le rogue'.

244. Norman *truté* 'caillé' (patois of Feugerolles-sur-Orne, C., Clécy, Thury-Harcourt, C. and La Ferrière-Hareng, Le Bény-Bocage, C.) *ALF,* Map 195, may be related to ON *þrútna* 'to swell'.

245. *Vittefleur* (S.-I.) may have as its first element ON *hvít-r* 'white'.

Miscellaneous Verbs

246. OF *aatir,* v. tr. 'défier, provoquer' has been traced to ON *at,* s.n. 'agitation, incitement' (cf. *etja,* v. tr. 'to incite', with the past tense *atta*) by the *FEW,* III, 248b and the *REW* 2920. Norm. *aratiné* in the expression *être aratiné de* is perhaps related, as is Prov. *adaptir,* cited by the *REW* 2920; the latter form makes it seem probable that the original ONorm. form was *adatir* (Lat. *ad* + ON *at*), since the spelling in *aa* was consistently used; cf. the derivatives: OF *aatie, aatine, aatison, aatise,* s.f. 'provocation', OF *aatisement,* s.m. 'provocation' and OF *aatiner,* v. tr. 'harceler'. However the *s* in the forms OF *aastie, aestie* (Godefroy, s.v. *aatie*) has not been explained, but is probably non-etymological.

247. ONorm. *bitter,* Norm. *biter,* v. tr. 'toucher, toucher à, se toucher (en parlant des billes, etc.), atteindre' is from ON *bíta* 'to bite, affect, make an impression' according to the *FEW,* I, 384. Cf. also ON *bíta* 'to extend, distend'. Among the derivatives are: OF *abiter* 'approcher' (12th c.); ONorm. *abiter* 'toucher à' (Orne, 1428); Norm. *abiter* 'toucher à'; Norm. *rabiter* 'toucher de nouveau'. The derivation of Fr. *bitte* 'membre viril' from this verb, supposedly contaminated with *habiter* in the expression *habiter avec ou à une femme,* in the *FEW,* I, 384, is rejected by Sjögren, pp. 386–7. Cf. above, §8.

248. Norm. *blikyi* 'loucher' (patois of the Manche) seems to be from ON *blika, blíkja* 'to gleam, twinkle' rather than from Eng. *blick* as stated in the *FEW,* I, 408, where no explanation

is given of how an English word of this type could have reached the continent. Cf. Norman *bllique* [bĺik] 'qui a un oeil plus grand que l'autre'.

249. Norman *crétir* 'frissonner' (patois of Le Havre, Bolbec, Pont-Audemer, Condé-sur-Noireau, C.); Norman *créter* (patois of Bayeux, Pont-Audemer) 'frissonner'; Norman *créti* (patois of La Hague) 'resserrer, rétrécir' is derived by the *FEW*, II, 608a,b, from Old Norse; W. von Wartburg mentions Swedish *kart* 'unripe fruit', Icelandic *karta* 'protuberance', and states that the Norman word comes from Old Norse with the idea of 'to shiver' based on the concept of goose-flesh. Phonetically, the change from [a] to [e] seems difficult, granting that metathesis did take place; ON had an expressive verb *kretta* 'to murmur' which may have played a part in the development of the Norman words, if they are of ON origin.

250. Fr. *écraser*, v. tr. 'to crush' has been traced to an ON word with the same meaning as Swedish *krasa* 'to crackle' and *krossa* 'to bruise, crush' (Dauzat, *DG*, s.v. *écraser;* Hellquist, s.v. *krasa*). The *REW* 4762 states that an ON **krasa* can only have given Fr. *écraser* through the intermediary of English *craze*; this latter word is of ON origin according to Hellquist, s.v. *krasa*. Falk-Torp, s.v. *kras*, sb. also give an ON source for the French and the English verbs. The difficulty caused by the late change of ON [s] to Fr. [z] is pointed out by Sainéan, *Les Sources indigènes de l'étymologie française*, II, 293. Falk-Torp, s.v. *kryste* mention an OF *cruisir* of Germanic origin. It may be that the voiced consonant in *écraser* resulted from contamination with the older Germanic loan *cruisir*. Cf. Thaon *ekrozae* (Guerlin de Guer, *Le Parler populaire de la commune de Thaon*, p. 40). The problem of *écraser* is far from solved; it is probably an expressive verb much older than the 10th century. Cf. the older form *accraser* (Huguet, s.v.).

250a. Norman *embarnir*, v. tr. 'rendre une femme enceinte' may be from ON, cf. OIcel. *barna*, v. tr. 'to get with child'. The Norman verb is listed by Moisy, *Glossaire*, and Du Bois, without any specific locality being mentioned. The word was extended to 'prendre de l'embonpoint' in which it is used reflexively in Norman, as in Old French. The OF verb *embarnir* 'prendre de l'embonpoint, grossir' seems to have been crossed with another OF verb *embarnir*, v. tr. 'rendre courageux' which was related to OF *barnage*, s.m. 'assemblée de barons; qualités d'un baron; courage, noblesse, etc.'. The forms [bàrnèt] [bàrnèz] 'jeune fille sans expérience' in the Pas de Calais (*ALF, Supplément*, I, 111a, Localities No. 284, 285) may be of West Germanic origin; cf. Old Saxon and OHG *barn* cited by Falk-Torp, s.v. *barn*, or may be from an unattested ONorm. *barn* that could have spread north on the coast.

251. Norman [énàkyé] (patois of Guernsey) 'avaler ce qui reste' (*ALF, Supplément*, I, 15b) may be from ON, cf. OIcel. *snaka* 'to rummage about'. Moisy, *Glossaire*, s.v. *enacs*, s.m. pl. 'restes d'un festin' likens the latter to English *snacks* but this is inaccurate for reasons of phonetic chronology, preconsonantal [s] in English words being retained in the patois of the Channel Islands. Cf. Jersey *sno* 'snuff' (*Glossaire du patois jersiais*).

252. OF *escraper*, v. tr. 'nettoyer en râclant' may be from ON, cf. OIcel. *skrapa* 'to scratch out' (Mackel, p. 139).

253. ONorm. *escriler, escriller,* Norman *griller, égriller, écriller* 'to slide' may be from ON *skriðla* 'to slide' reconstructed on the basis of Swedish dialectal *skrilla* 'to skate'; Hellquist, s.v. *skrilla* derives this from *skriðla*; the ON etymology of the Fr. words is in Hopfgarten, pp. 31–32; Dauzat and Bloch, s.v. *égrillard*. ONorm. *escriller* occurred in the *Roman de Rou* (Godefroy, s.v. *escriller*). Cf. also Norman [à fè dz égriõ] 'on glisse' (patois of Orbec, C.) *ALF, Supplément*, I, 271a, Locality No. 343.

254. ONorm. *esneier*, v. tr. 'déblayer, débarrasser' in Benoît's *Chronique des ducs de Normandie* and *Les Quatre Livres des rois* (Moisy, *Glossaire*, s.v. *esneier*) may be from ON, cf. OIcel. *sneyða* 'to bereave one of'.

255. ONorm. *esterchir*, v. refl. 's'affermir' may be from ON *sterk-r, sterk* 'strong'. Two of the three examples cited by Godefroy are from Robert Wace. The *REW* 8247 derives the word from Frankish, however. Cf. also A. Thomas, *Nouveaux Essais de philologie française*, p. 265. Cf. OIcel. *styrkja* 'to make strong'.

256. Norm. *eyer* 'regarder, voir, observer' may be from ON *eygja* 'to look'. The Norm. word is in Moisy, *Glossaire*.

257. Fr. *flâner* 'to lounge about', ONorm. *flâner* 'aller sans but en se laissant distraire par une chose ou par une autre pour passer le temps', 1645; Norm. *flâner* 'perdre son temps à causer, au lieu de travailler' are from ON *flana* 'to rush heedlessly' (*FEW*, III, 604–5; *REW* 3353a; Bloch, Dauzat, s.v. *flâner*). The word is very common in Normandy with many derived forms: *fllāon* 'bavardage', *flanée* 'causerie familière', *flânier* 'cancanier', *fllagné* 'bavard', *fllannette* 'femme babillarde', *fllanneter* 'babiller', etc. Derived forms in standard French are: *flâne* 'flânerie', 1856; *flânerie,* 16th c. 'action de flâner'; *flâneur* 'celui qui flâne' also since the 16th c.

258. ONorm. *flatir*, v.i. 'être jeté à plat' in Wace, *Roman de Brut* may be from ON *flat-r,* adj. 'flat'. Cf. Eng. *flat* also of ON origin (Falk-Torp, s.v. *flad*).

259. Norm. *floner*, v.r. 'se pâmer de colère ou de surprise', Norm. *flonné* 'irrité', Norm. *flonise* 'pâmoison par l'effet d'une grande colère' are from ON *flóna* 'to become warm' according to the *FEW*, III, 627b, where it is added that ON *flon* 'fool' may also be considered.

260. ONorm. *gaber*, v. tr. 'se moquer de' is from ON *gabba* 'to mock' (Dauzat, Bloch, *DG*, s.v. *gaber*; Hopfgarten, p. 75; *REW* 3626, and *OED*, s.v. *gab*, sb. 1). Among the many nouns formed from the same root in OF may be cited the following with the meaning 'moquerie, plaisanterie': *gabe, gab, gabel(e), gabelet, gabement, gaberi(s)e, gabesse, gabet, gabil, gaboi(e), gabois(on)*. Cf. also OF *gabeler* 'se moquer de'. OF *gaber*, first attested in the *Chanson de Roland*, was reintroduced into literary French ca. 1860. Cf. also ONorm. *gabeux* 'farceurs' used by D. Ferrand, V, 100.

261. Norm. *gnaquer* 'mordre' has been derived by Joret, p. 94, from ON *gnaga* 'to gnaw', an etymology accepted by Nyrop, *Grammaire historique*, I, 18 but rejected by Sainéan, *Les Sources indigènes de l'étymologie française*, II, 294 because the root is found in various Germanic languages. Another objection to the ON etymology is the passing of [gn] to [ñ] after 900. Cf. also Norm. *gniaquée*, s.f. 'morsure de chien' (Du Bois).

262. Norm. *grā* 'vêtir' (Alderney, Guernsey, Sark, *ALF* Map 1381, *ALF Supplément*, I, 102c), also spelt *grâie* (Métivier) seems to be from ON *greiða* 'to arrange, make ready'. Cf. §1.

263. ONorm., Norm. *haguer*, v. tr. 'hacher, déchiqueter' seems to be from an ODan. *°hagga*, cf. OIcel. *hǫggva* 'to hew'. Cf. Norm. *hague*, s.f. 'un des morceaux de bois . . . qui composent le fagot' (D. Ferrand, V, 115). The Norm. verb is listed by Moisy, *Glossaire*; Métivier, Decorde and Duméril.

264. Fr. *hanter*, v. tr. 'to haunt, frequent' has been derived from ON *heimta* 'to recover, get home sheep from summer pastures, to claim' by Bloch, Dauzat and the *DG*, s.v. *hanter*. An ODan. *°hemta* would better explain Fr. *hanter* phonetically. The word, which was first attested in the 12th c. had many OF derivatives: OF *hant, hantage, hantance, hantie* 'fréquentation, hantise', OF *hantin* 'séjour'; among the modern forms are: *hantement* 'hantise', *hantise* 'fréquentation'. Cf. Norm. *hanter* 'fréquenter, especialement en vue de mariage' (Maze, patois of Le Havre). Cf. *ALF*, Map 563, Localities 361, 371, 378 and 387 for similar forms.

265. Fr. *harper*, v. tr. 'to grip, clutch' is probably the result of contamination of Lat. *harpe* 'sickle' with an ON word similar to Icel. *harpa* 'to pinch'. AN *harpon* was attested in the 12th c. and in the 14th c. the word-family was limited to Picardy and to Anglo-Norman, surviving today in western France. These factors, together with the aspirate [h] which could not come from Latin without Germanic influence, make the ON origin probable. Fr. *harper* 'to grip' existed from the 12th–18th c. but survives as Norm. *harper* 'saisir' (Duméril, Du Bois, Decorde). The ON etymology is given by the *FEW*, IV, 388–9 and by Bloch, s.v. *harpon*.

266. *héler*, v. tr. 'to hail', first attested in 1527, is according to the *DG* and Bloch from English *to hail*. However, the latter was not attested until 1563 in the sense 'to call to a ship from a distance' (*OED*, s.v. *hail*, v. 2) and is itself of ON origin, ultimately from the ON noun *heill* 'health'. It may be accidental that the French word was attested first, but the possibility of direct ON origin for the French word cannot be overlooked.

267. Western Fr. *hucher*, v. refl. 'to perch' seems to be from ON *húka*, v.i. 'to squat'. Fr. *hucher* seems to be a word independent of *jucher* 'to perch' (< Frankish *juk). Cf. the *REW* 4611.

268. Norman [kłape] 'battre des mains' (patois of Guernsey), in the *ALF, Supplément*, I, 21a, is either from ON *klappa* 'to pat, rap, stroke gently' or from English *clap*.

269. Norman [mẽšyi] 'briser' may be from ON *minnka* 'to diminish'. The word is in the *ALF, Supplément*, I, 30a, Locality No. 399 (Guernsey). Cf. also Norman *bro*, s.m. 'déchirure' (patois of Jersey, *Glossaire du patois jersiais*, s.v. *bro*) which may be ON *brot*, s.n. 'breaking, fragment, etc.'.

270. Norman *ransaquer*, v. tr. 'to ransack' (patois of Guernsey) may be from ON, cf. OIcel. *rann-saka* 'to ransack'; English *ransack* is also of ON origin. The Guernsey word is listed in Métivier and in Moisy, *Glossaire*, s.v. *ransaquer*.

271. *regretter*, OF *regrater*, first attested in *Alexis* in the 11th century and originally meaning in OF 'se lamenter sur un mort' may be from ON, cf. OIcel. *gráta* 'to weep, bewail, weep for one' with possible influence of ON *gretta* 'to frown'. An ON etymology is given by the *DG*, Dauzat and Bloch, s.v. *regretter*. Bloch states that the presence of the prefix *re-* is not clear. Fr. *regret* is attested in the 12th c.

272. Norman *winé* 'pleurer' (patois of Thaon, C.) listed by Guerlin de Guer, *Le Parler populaire de la commune de Thaon*, p. 400; Bas Maine *gwiné*; Norman *ouiné* (patois of Bessin) 'gémir en parlant des chiens' cited by Guerlin de Guer, p. 400; these words may be from Old Norse; cf. OIcel. *veina* 'to wail', ODan. *hvine* 'to neigh, bray'; English *whine* < ON (Hellquist, s.v. *vina*).

Other Words of Possible Old Norse Origin in
French and Norman

273. Norman *badé*, adj. 'couvert de boue ou d'eau' (patois of Orne) is traced by Duméril to ON, cf. OIcel. *baða* 'to bathe'. Du Bois lists a reflexive verb *se bader* 'mouiller ses vêtements par le bas'.

274. Norman *bllâse* [blãs] 'brouillard' (patois of Guernsey) is derived by the *FEW*, I, 402a, from English *blase* 'blasen'; the word is more probably from ON, cf. OIcel. *blása* 'to blow' used of the wind; the past participle *blásinn* meant 'stripped of turf, bare, barren'. The intervocalic [s] of the Guernsey word could hardly have come from an English [z].

275. ONorm. *buc*, s.m. 'buste, tronc' in the *Chanson de Roland* and the *Chronique des ducs de Normandie* (cf. Moisy, *Glossaire*, s.v. *buc* 2) may be from ON, cf. OIcel. *búk-r*, s.m. 'body, trunk'. The *FEW*, I, 600a-602 derives *buc* from Frankish *°būk* 'Bauch'.

276. *but*, s.m. 'goal', OF *but*, s.m. 'pièce de vêtement' may be from ON *bút-r* 'stump' (*REW* 1424a). The *FEW*, I, 653a, gives a Frankish source, but W. von Wartburg adds that the word is almost exclusively Norman during the 12th and 13th centuries. The semantic development is explained by the fact that blocks of wood were used as targets in the shooting of the crossbow and the bow and arrow. For the many derivatives of this word, see the *FEW*, I, 653a.

277. *caque*, s.f. 'herring-barrel' may be from ON *kaggi*, s.m. 'keg, cask' (cf. Valkhoff, s.v. *caque*). The word may have been associated with *caquer* 'préparer les harengs pour les mettre en caque', which is of Dutch origin.

278. Norman *drigo*, s.m. 'boisson' (patois of Guernsey) may be from ODan. *°drikka* 'to drink' (cf. Danish *drikke*, OIcel. *drekka*). ONorm. *dragler* 'to drink' used by David Ferrand in the 17th century (cf. ed. A. Héron, V, 67) may be from Old Norse; cf. OIcel. *draga* 'to draw (i.e. liquids from a barrel), to drink';. cf. English *draught, draft* 'the drawing of a liquid from its receptacle' and also 'drink'.

279. ONorm. *escharir* 'effarer, effrayer' in Wace's *Roman
de Rou* (cf. Moisy, *Glossaire*, s.v. *escharir*) may be from Old
Norse. The *OED*, s.v. *scare*, vb. traces the English word to
Old Norse and mentions OIcel. *skirra* 'to frighten' and *skjarr*
'timid'. ONorm. *escharir* may have a similar ON origin.

280. ONorm. *esterchir* (see §255).

281. *furolle,* s.f. 'jack o' lantern, will o' the wisp'; MFr.
fuirolle (1549, 1771) 'feu follet'; also *fuyrolle, furole, fourolle*;
furole (patois of Yères, Bray, Tôtes, Le Havre, Pont-Audemer),
furolles (patois of Louviers) 'feux que l'on allume dans la
campagne la nuit de Noël ou des rois'; *furoller* (patois of Louviers) 'faire brûler des furolles'; *furole* (patois of Le Havre)
'cheval ombrageux et craintif' are derived in the *FEW*, III,
929b from Anglo-Saxon *fyr* 'fire'; W. von Wartburg states
that ON *fúr-r* does not explain the *ui* of the earlier forms;
there was also an ON *fýr-r* 'fire', however.

282. Fr. *gable*, s.f. 'gable' is derived by Falk-Torp from
ON *gafl*, s.m. 'gable' (s.v. *gavl*). The word occurred in Normandy in 1338 (Dauzat, s.v. *gable*) and English *gable* is
also believed to be of ON origin. However, if OF *jable*, s.m.
'réunion à leur sommet de deux pièces de bois inclinées, couronnement triangulaire d'un mur, pignon d'un portail, d'une
fenêtre' (Godefroy, *Lexique*) is the same word, then a source
older than the Norse settlement of Neustria must be found.
The *FEW*, IV, 17b, gives a Celtic origin for these words.

283. Norman *gadel* 'gooseberry' (patois of the Seine-Inférieure) has been derived from ON, cf. OIcel. *gadd-r*, gen.
gadds, s.m. 'goad, spike' by Joret, *Romania*, VIII (1879),
440, and listed in the *REW* 3632; the etymology is explained
by the prickly surface of the gooseberry. Difficulty, however,
is caused by the fact that most of the Norman forms have [r];
gradil (patois of Guernsey and Calvados); *grad* (patois of
Calvados); *kadr* (patois of Manche); *gard* (patois of S.-I.);
gadel occurs not only in Normandy, but also in Eure-et-Loir,
Seine-et-Oise and the Sarthe; *garzile* 'groseiller' is found in the
Pas de Calais. (Cf. *ALF*, Maps No. 670 and 671).

284. *gerfaut*, s.m. 'gerfalcon' which the *REW* 3713 derives
from ON, cf. OIcel. *geirfalki* causes difficulty because we would

expect [g] in a word of ON origin. The ON etymology is also given by Baist, *Romania*, XII (1883), 99–100, and is in *Mélanges linguistiques offerts à Gaston Paris*, p. 531.

285. Fr. *hagard*, adj. 'haggard'; OF *hagart* 'incertain, changeant', but also originally used to describe the untrained bird in falconry, as still in *faucon hagard*. Ménagier's etymology *esprevier hagart est celluy qui est de mue de hayes*, i.e., 'qui demeure pendant la mue dans les haies' is considered a popular etymology by Bloch, s.v. *hagard*. However, the fact that Ménagier associated *hagart* with *haie* may mean that it was derived from an ONorm. *hague* 'enclos, haie' listed by Godefroy, *Lexique*; this would probably be of ON origin; cf. OIcel. *hagi* 'pasture, field for grazing'. The word *hagard* could not be much older than the Viking invasion; otherwise [g] would not have remained.

286. AN *hansac*, s.m. 'coutelas, poignard' may be from ON, cf. OIcel. *hand-sax*, s.n. 'short sword, dagger' rather than from Anglo-Saxon *handseax*, as stated by W. von Wartburg in the *ZRPh.*, LXIII (1943), 216, who also rejects the OHG etymology in the *REW* 4029. The word also appeared as *hansart* in Old Norman with suffix change.

287. Norman *hatie*, s.f. (Moisy, *Glossaire*); Norman *hati*, s.m. 'hatred' (Duméril) may be from ON, cf. OIcel. *hata* 'to hate' with a Romance ending.

288. *hautbar* 'dicentrarchus labrax' attested since 1671, is derived by Paul Barbier, *RLR*, LVIII (1915) 309, from ON, cf. OIcel. *haf* 'sea' plus *bar* (cf. Danish *aborre* with mutated vowel). Le Héricher, *Glossaire*, I, 154, cites *bars* and *sabars* as names of fishes in the *Roman de Mont-Saint-Michel*. W. von Wartburg, *FEW*, I, 266b, rejects Barbier's etymology, stating that it implies that ON *haf* survived for a time in Normandy as an independent word.

289. ONorm., OF *hait, heit*, s.m. 'joie, plaisir, gré', OF *deshait* 'découragement', Norman *déhé* (patois of Val de Saire, La Hague); Norman *dég'houet* (patois of Guernsey) have been derived by Sjögren, p. 400, from ON *heit*, s.n. 'promise, vow'; Hopfgarten, p. 41, also traces OF *hait* to Old Norse. This

etymology, however, is not generally accepted. Cf. Bloch, s.v. *souhaiter*.

290. Norman [hūvá] 'nourriture grossière' (patois of Guernsey) in the *ALF*, *Supplément*, I, 6, s.v. *alimentation* may be from ON, cf. OIcel. *hóf*, s.n. 'feast, banquet'.

291. ONorm. *lage*, s.f. 'règlement, loi, coutume'< ODan. °*lag* (cf. OIcel. *lǫg*, s.n. pl. and English *law* of ON origin). The word is used in Wace's *Roman de Brut* (cf. Moisy, *Glossaire*, s.v. *lage*).

292. Norman *léican*, s.m. 'benêt' (Duméril), 'nigaud' (Du Bois) has been derived by Duméril from ON, cf. OIcel. *leika* 'to play'. W. von Wartburg, *FEW*, I, vi, gives *léican* as a word of unknown origin. The *ALF*, *Supplément*, I, 8a, gives the Norman form [l'ékā] 'l'amusement' for Guernsey.

293. Northern Fr. [mwargunē] 'rhume de cerveau' (patois of Liège and northern Luxemburg) is derived by Jean Haust, *ZRPh*, LVII (1937), 374, from ON *morkinn*, ODan. *morken* 'rotten'. No explanation is given of how the words became limited to that area without any apparent forms in use in Normandy.

294. Fr. *nantir*, v. tr. 'to pledge', OF *nant* 'gage'<ON, cf. OIcel. *nám*, s.n. 'seizure, occupation' (Bloch, s.v. *nantir*). The word occurred in the LL of England as *namum, namium,* and survives in Normandy as *namps*, s.m. pl. 'gage, nantissement' (Duméril); at Guernsey, the word *namps* means 'gage, meuble' and at Jersey the word means 'effets saisis par l'officier de Justice' (*Glossaire du patois jersiais*, s.v. *namps*). In the patois of the Manche, [il ō fe le naōtiz] means 'ils sont fiancés' (*ALF*, Map No. 563, Locality No. 358). The ON etymology is also given by Hopfgarten, p. 64, but Dauzat, s.v. *nantir* and the *REW* 5817a, as well as Gamillscheg, 633a derive the word from Frankish.

295. Norman *rimer*, v.i. 'geler à blanc'; Norman *rimée*, s.f. 'gelée blanche'; ONorm. (16th century, Cotentin) *rimasser*, a frequentative form of *rimer*< ON, cf. OIcel. *hrím*, ODan. °*rīm* 'hoar-frost'. These words are listed by Moisy, *Glossaire* and Du Bois. Cf. the much older Germanic loan *frimas* taken into Gallo-Roman when Germanic initial [hr] was treated as

Romance initial [fr], with sound substitution.

296. OF *targe*, s.f. 'shield' is derived by the *OED*, s.v. *targe* from ON, cf. OIcel. *targa*, s.f. 'target, small round shield'; the same etymology is in Hopfgarten, p. 35. A phonetic difficulty is caused by the fact that ON [g] should have remained as [g] in ON words integrated into the Romance of Normandy. On the other hand, English *target* with [g] seems to come from an ONorm. *targue, which could be of ON origin.

Medieval and Modern Borrowings from the Scandinavian Languages

For the sake of completeness, loans from the Scandinavian languages which do not date back to the Viking settlement of Normandy will be treated here. Words such as *ibsénisme*, *swedenborgisme* and *abélien* have not been included, since they are obviously French creations, nor have words created by Scandinavian scientists from Greek or Latin roots (*brachycéphale, dynamite*), nor have words like *fonctionnel, médium* and *sextant*, non-Scandinavian words which have acquired special meanings in Scandinavia and which were then introduced into French.

297. Literary Terms: *Ases*, s.m. pl. 'dieux de la mythologie scandinave qui représent les forces de la nature' (*Larousse*), used by Leconte de Lisle in "Légende des Nornes"; *edda*, s.m. 'mot qui sert à indiquer deux recueils des traditions mythologiques et légendaires des anciens peuples scandinaves'; *Norne*, s.f. 'Norn', like *edda* has been admitted by the Academy; *rune*, s.f. 'rune', attested in French in 1670, in English in 1690; *runique*, adj. 'runic'; *saga*, s.f. 'saga', admitted by the Academy; *scalde*, s.m. 'scald', admitted by the Academy; *scaldique*, adj. 'scaldic'.

298. Historical and Geographical Terms: *banquise*, s.f. 'énorme amas de glaces côtières, résultant de la congélation de l'eau de la mer', perhaps a contamination of Dan. *pakis* lit. 'pack of ice' with Fr. 'banc de glace', rather than from English (Barbier, *English Influence on the French Vocabulary*) or German *Eisbank* (Dauzat); *drakkar*, s.m. 'bateau des pirates

normands' (*Larousse*); *fiord*, s.m. 'fjord' late 19th c. (Bloch) <
Norw. *fjord*, attested in English in 1674 (*OED*); *geyser*, s.m. 'geyser', attested in 1812, but in 1780 in English; *iarl*, *jarl*, s.m. 'jarl,
earl' used by Victor Hugo in *Han d'Islande* and Leconte de Lisle
in *Poèmes barbares; lur*, s.m. 'longue trompe de bronze des anciens danois', *Larousse Mensuel Illustré*, II (1911) 212; *snékar*,
s.m. 'grand bateau dont se servaient les pirates normands pour
remonter la Seine' (*Nouveau Larousse Universel*); *tjäle*, s.m.
'terme de morphologie arctique désignant la partie du sol per-
pétuellement gelée' (< Swed. *tjäle*), listed in the *Larousse
Mensuel Illustré*, XII (1948–51) 206; *varangues*, *varangiens*,
s.m. pl. 'soldats mercénaires d'origine franque ou normande qui
composaient la garde particulière des empereurs byzantins'
(*Nouveau Larousse Universel*), cf. Swed. *väring; varve*, s.f.
'ensemble de deux couches, l'une argileuse, l'autre sableuse et
plus claire, déposées par les eaux de fonte d'un glacier', *Larousse Mensuel Illustré*, XII (1948–51), 256, probably from
Swed. *varv* 'layer'; *viking*, s.m. 'viking', *Nouveau Larousse Illustré*.

299.   Animals, Birds, Fishes, etc.: *aspe*, s.m. 'Aspius rapax'
from Lat. *Aspius* created by Linnaeus from Swed. *asp* (Hellquist, s.v. *asp*, 1); *brosme*, s.m. 'type of shellfish' used by Lacé-
pède, cf. Paul Barbier, *RDR*, I (1909), 433; *édredon*, s.m.
'eider-down, eider-down quilt', attested in 1700, probably from
Swed. *eiderdun* (*FEW*, III, 208a); *eider*, s.m. 'eider-duck'
1771 (*FEW*, III, 208a), cf. OF *edre*, 13th–16th c. which was
reintroduced as *eider; harfang*, s.m. 'harfang, Great Snowy Owl'
attested in 1760 as *harfaong* (*DG*), attested in English in 1774
(*OED*), from Swed. *harfång; ide*, s.m. 'genre de poissons télé-
ostéens. . . .' in the *Nouveau Larousse Universel* from Lat.
idus, formed by Linnaeus from Swed. *id* 'Leuciscus idus' (Hellquist, s.v. *id*, 1); *lemming*, s.m. 'genre de mammifères rongeurs
. . . répandus dans le nord de l'Europe' (*Larousse*) from Dan.
or Swed. dial. *lemming* (Hellquist, s.v. *lämmel*); *lumme, lumne*,
s.m. 'genre d'oiseaux palmipèdes. . . .' (*Larousse*) is ultimately
from Swed. or Dan. *lom*, but perhaps from Eng. *loom*, attested
in 1694 (*OED*, s.v. *loom*, sb. 2); *narval*, s.m. 'narwhal', attested
in 1663 as *narhual* (Ch. Patin who quotes a Danish work, cf.
Bloch), in Furetière as *narwal*, attested in English in 1658

(*OED*, s.v. *narwhal*); *ranger, rangier*, s.m. 'reindeer' attested
in the 13th c.; according to E. Richter, 191–2, n. 10 it could
not have come directly from Norse without passing through a
West Germanic language; however, an ODan. [-diur] would have
given Fr. [-dier], influenced by Fr. words in *-gier; renne*, s.m.
'reindeer', attested in 1552 in a translation of a German work, was
believed by Nyrop, *Romania*, XXXV (1906), 563, n. 3 to be directly from Norw. or Swed. *ren; rorqual*, s.m. 'rorqual, finback'
(< Norw. *røyrkval*), Eng. *rorqual* probably of Fr. origin (*OED*);
the change from [hv-] to [kv-] did not take place in Iceland and
Norway until long after 900, so the word must be recent; *rutabaga*, s.m. 'plante du genre chou, dite navet de Suède, cultivée
surtout pour l'alimentation des animaux domestiques' (*DG*) from
Swed. dial. *rotabagge* (Bloch, *DG*), first attested in France in
1803, appears in the Marne as *ruta* and as *tabaga* in Pas de Calais
and Maine-et-Loire (*ALF, Supplément*, I, 199b); the *u* in Fr.
rutabaga has not been explained.

300.   Ski Terms, Sports, etc.: *anorak*, s.m. 'vareuse fourrée
à capuchon', listed in the *Larousse Mensuel Illustré*, XII (1948–
51), 81 and *Vie et langage*, XII (1953), 138, originally an Es-
kimo word used in Danish, used by André Martinet in spoken
French as early as 1934; *bakken*, s.m. 'piste de saut, tremplin'
from Norw. *bakken* 'the hill', also 'springboard' (Gredig, p.
31); *christiania, christi*, s.m. 'coup d'arrêt' from the former name
of Oslo (Gredig, pp. 36–37, Dauzat); *fart*, s.m. 'enduit dont
on imprègne les skis pour les rendre plus glissants' from Norw.
fart 'trip' used to indicate the product in question (cf. also
farter 'enduire de fart' and *farteur*, s.m. 'appareil à l'aide duquel
on farte les skis à chaud', Gredig, pp. 46–47); *kjelke*, s.m. 'petit
traîneau norvégien qui se gouverne à l'aide d'une perche', <
Norw. *kjelke* 'sleigh' (*Larousse*); *laupar*, s.m. 'soulier spécial
pour le ski' (< Norw. *lauparsko* 'skier's shoe'), formerly used
in French, cf. *Vie et langage*, II (1953), 87; *ski*, s.m. 'ski', listed
by Littré in 1876 as *skie*, s.f., appeared in the *Magasin pittoresque*
in 1841, and in the form *skidders* in La Mortraye's *Voyage en
Europe, Asie et Afrique*; cf. also *skiable*, adj., *skiage*, s.m. only
used in the program of the 1912 Olympic games, *skier* 'to ski'

replaced by *faire du ski*; *skieur, skieuse*, s.m. & f. (cf. Gredig, pp. 59–63); *slalom*, s.m. 'descente en zigzag en ski' (< Norw. *slalom*) appeared in 1910 in French, and in 1912 in a work translated from Norwegian (Gredig, pp. 63–65); cf. also *slalomeur*, s.m. 'person who performs a *slalom*', and *descente slalomisée* 'descente ou piste de descente aménagée de façon à être dévalée en slalom'; *pas de stavhugg*, s.m. 'pas de course de fond . . . dont la technique consiste à exécuter deux ou trois glissés en amenant les bâtons simultanément en avant' from Norw. *stavhugg* (Gredig, p. 56); *télémark, télé*, s.m. 'virage-arrêt en trace serrée en position fendue et avec plus ou moins de vissage de corps' from the Norw. place-name *Telemark* (Gredig, p. 69).

301. *éberguer*, v. tr. 'préparer (la morue) en l'ouvrant, la vidant. etc., et la traînant à la remorque du bateau pêcheur' (*DG*) is said to be from the particle *é* + *Bergen*, the Norwegian city from where this preparation comes (*DG*, Dauzat, *FEW*, I, 333a). The construction of the word, first attested in Littré, is rather unusual for a recent loan. To explain the prefix, the *FEW* states: "Das Präfix findet seine sachliche Rechtfertigung darin, dass bei dieser Art Zubereitung der Stockfische die Tiere ausgeweidet werden".

Addenda

Several Norman words of ON origin are listed in the *FEW* XVI: ONorm. *gomer* 'palais' < ON *gómr* 'Gaumen'; Norm. *hannes* 'culotte'< ON *hamr* 'Gewand'; Norm. *hāonseire* 'manchot' < ON *hand-sarr* 'wund an der Hand'; Norm. *haitier* 'large poêle à frire. . . .'< ON *heitr* 'hot'; OF *hustin* 'bruit'< ON *húsþing* 'meeting, assembly'. However the development of ON *hju* 'Diener, Mannschaft' to MFr. *ohie* 'faiblesse' is phonetically and semantically difficult to accept, as is the development of ON *hrota* to Pic. *crot*, there being no example of ON [h-] replaced by OF [k-]. Such a change was impossible in the 10th century.

FOOTNOTES

[1]For example, Edélestand and Alfred Duméril, *Dictionnaire du patois normand* (Caen, 1849). The work was severely criticized by Z. Collin, *Lund Universitets Årsskrift* (1864), 3rd art.

[2]Jean Adigard des Gautries, *Les noms de personnes scandinaves en Normandie de 911 à 1066*, Nomina Germanica 11 (Lund, 1954).

[3]Friedrich Diez, *Grammatik der romanischen Sprachen*. 2nd ed., (Bonn, 1856) I, 65.

[4]A number of Norse etymologies proposed by Vising, Schuchardt, Braune, Brüch, Baist and Jud were justly rejected by Meyer-Lübke in the *REW* for phonetic or semantic reasons.

[5]Cf. Charles Joret, *Des caractères et de l'extension du patois normand* (Paris, 1883) and also *Les Noms de lieu d'origine non romane et la colonisation scandinave et germanique en Normandie* (Rouen, 1913).

[6]It is unfortunate that the most recent edition of the *DG* includes an introduction which, the editors state, represents their definitive opinion. In this list (I, 18) *bateau, fret* and *lof* are given as Fr. words of ON origin, whereas in the dictionary proper more accurate information is given under the respective words. Moreover, on p. 19, Fr. *elfe* 'elf' is wrongly given as a word of ON origin.

[7]Cf. J. A. des Gautries, pp. 15–16 for a criticism of Pedersen.

[8]Cf. also the German version "Ein vermeintliches Wikingerwort", *Wörter und Sachen*, VII (Heidelberg, 1921), 81–101.

[9]O. Bloch & W. von Wartburg, *Dictionnaire étymologique de la langue française* (Paris, 1950), p. xxx.

[10]We consider this statement false, of course, and shall seek to prove that the Norse influence on the French vocabulary has been considerable.

[11]Peter Skautrup, *Det Danske Sprogs Historie*, I, 124–5.

[12]Skautrup, I, 47.

[13]In the present study we shall use the term Old Danish where Björkman uses East Scandinavian, and Old Norwegian for West Scandinavian.

[14]Cf. Robert L. Politzer, "On the Chronology of the Simplification of Geminates in Northern France", *Modern Language Notes*, Dec. 1951, pp. 527–531.

[15]André Martinet, *Language* XXVIII (Baltimore, 1952), p. 205.

[16]Pope, p. 169, states that the audible nasalization of the low vowels began first with [ã] and [ãi] in the 10th century.

[17]The OIcel. forms will be quoted when there is no reason to believe that the ODan. form differed from it. The spelling of the OIcel. forms is largely taken from F. Holthausen, *Vergleichendes und etymologisches Wörterbuch des Altwestnordischen*. The advantage of this spelling is that the flexional ending is separated from the root by a hyphen, e.g. *bekk-r* 'brook' is given rather than *bekkr*, the form found in many other dictionaries.

[18]Cf. n. 14.

[19]Cf. Pope, p. 98.

[20]Cf. Pope, p. 125 and p. 128.

[21]Cf. A. Sjögren, *Romania*, LIV (1928), 405.

[22]Cf. Sjögren, p. 383, n. 2.

[23]See the *REW*, §7965b, and Falk-Torp, s.v. *skaffe*.

[24]OIcel. *f* represents [v] in *bifa*.

[25]Pope, p. 140, states that in intervocalic position between homophonous vowels [ð] began to be effaced in eastern and north-eastern France in the late 9th century. In final position in this region [þ] began to be effaced before homophonous consonants in the same period, but in the west the process was later. The complete absence of elision of the unstressed termination [-þ] in the *Alexis* and the continued use of the analogical forms *sed, qued, ned* in this poem, indicate the maintenance of final [þ] and [ð] in Normandy in the middle of the 11th century.

[26]J. A. des Gautries, pp. 156, 424, 425. Cf. also ON *þormoðr* > *Turmodus* > *Tormodivilla, Tormot villa, Tormovilla* > *Tourmauville* (pp. 166-7).

[27]J. A. des Gautries, pp. 135-6.

[28]There was also an OIcel. *mann-r* in early texts. Cf. Cleasby-Vigfusson s.v. *maðr*.

[29]Cf. E. Ekwall, *The Oxford Book of English Place-Names*, s.v. *Thorganby*, and *passim* under words in *Tor-*.

[30]J. A. des Gautries, *Annales de Normandie*, I (1951), 39-40.

[31]Cf. Pope, p. 217.

[32]Björkman, pp. 301-2 states that ON [s] normally was equated with Eng. [s], but it appears to have become voiced according to the same rules as native [s] as in Eng. *raise* and Eng. dial. *oozely* 'miserable' (< ON *úsall, úsæll*).

[33]Another possible explanation of the change from [s] to [z] in the Norman names is the fact that many of the Vikings came to Neustria from England, where such a change was normal, rather than directly from Scandinavia. Cf. J. A. des Gautries, pp. 268-270.

[34]Cf. *ALF*, Map No. 684, locality No. 351.

[35]Cf. Jakob Jakobsen, *An Etymological Dictionary of the Norn Language in Shetland*, II, s.v. *sjarl*.

[36]Cf. Pope, pp. 153-5.

[37]Paul Barbier, *Zeitschrift für neufranzösische Sprache und Literatur*, LIII (1929), 7 states that [l] had normally fallen before [m] in Norman words.

[38]Gunnar Tilander, *Studia neophilologica*, XXIII (1950-1), 145-149 states that *Guillaume* is from ON *Wilhjalm* with [ja] instead of West Germanic [e]. This is supported by the fact that in eastern France the same proper name has the forms *Guillerme* and *Vuillerme*, which are of West Germanic origin.

[39]J. A. des Gautries, pp. 92-93, 400-1, 406-8, 410, 414-5.

[40]See also Paul Barbier, *RLR*, LXVII, 323-4.

[41]J. A. des Gautries, *Annales de Normandie*, II (1952), 31.

[42]Cited by Pope, p. 157.

[43]E. Richter, p. 247. Cf. also *meon* for *meum* in the *Oaths of Strasbourg*.

[44]At the time when ODan. words were taken into Romance, it would seem that [m] could not occur in final position in the latter language, having been neutralized to [n]. Thus when derivatives were formed from a form such as ONorm. *run,* either [m] or [n] was liable to be used. Cf. *arumer* and *arruner*.

[45]Bloch, s.v. *étrave*.

[46]J. A. des Gautries, pp. 77–78.

[47]Sjögren, p. 394, suggests that the nominative *hún-n* was borrowed; this would account for the final vowel in *hune*. To explain *grune*, Sjögren, p. 393, states that ON [-nn] represented a longer and probably more intense phoneme than Romance [-n] at the time of the Viking colonization. Sjögren believed that an ON word in [-nn] pronounced by Romance speakers would be followed by an off-glide and thus grouped with words of the feminine gender in [-ne].

[48]Professor André Martinet called to my attention such a possibility by pointing to the lenition of intervocalic [m] to [v].

[49]Cf. F. Lechanteur, *Annales de Normandie*, III (1953), 194.

[50]Cf. *Coutumiers de Normandie*, ed. Ernest-Joseph Tardif, II, 50.

[51]In 1066 the Normans must have had [w-] and [gw-] in Germanic words, to judge by the French words taken into English.

[52]The area using initial [g-] (from earlier [gw-]) has now extended from Paris over a large part of Normandy. The area with [w-] seems to be limited to only a few localities, while the area with initial [v-] is still large. To cite a word which is not of ON origin, Fr. *guêpe*, a word of Latin origin influenced by Germanic, has [v-] in the northern part of the Manche, Calvados, Seine-Inférieure and the northern part of the Eure, while the southern part of the Eure and the Manche, a large part of Calvados and all of the Orne have [g-] today (*ALF*, Map No. 672). *ALF* Map 575 shows a similar pattern for Fr. *gui* but with initial [w-] in La Frenaye, Lillebonne, S.-I. Guerlin de Guer, *Le Parler populaire dans la commune de Thaon (Calvados)*, p. 400 recorded the pronunciation [winé] whereas [gwiné] is the form used in Bas Maine for 'to weep'.

[53]J. A. des Gautries, *Annales de Normandie*, I (1951), 25, 42–43; III (1953), 28, 145–6.

[54]F. Lechanteur, *Annales de Normandie*, I (1951), 105, n. 1 writes: "On trouve [v] pour [g] dans tout le domaine proprement normand, mais de façon assez irrégulière et ne touchant que quelques rares mots. . . ."

[55]Cf. F. Falc'hun, *Le Système consonantique du breton* (Rennes, 1951), p. 84ff for a discussion of Celtic lenition.

[56]Cf. Pope, p. 78 and pp. 96–97.

[57]Cf. *FEW*, III, 236a, where no mention is made of the fact that ON *jord* had the genitive *jardar*.

[58]*FEW*, III, 63a, and Hellquist, s.v. *deja*.

[59]Pope, p. 173.

[60]Cf. J. A. des Gautries, *Annales de Normandie*, III (1953), 23.

[61]Pope, p. 79 and p. 112.

[62]Björkman, p. 295.

[63]Cf. Fritz Askeberg, *Namn och Bygd*, XXXII (1944), 176–203. Askeberg has shown, pp. 187–8, that the first appearance of forms with [ie], e.g. *Guiercia*, coincides chronologically with the change of *virge* > *vierge* and *cirge* > *cierge*.

[64]For the later development of [ǫ] and [ọ] in French, cf. George R. Shipman, *The Vowel Phonemes of Meigret*, pp. 47–59.

[65]P. Fouché, *Revue internationale d'onomastique*, IV (1952), 161ff.

[66]See Haudricourt and Juilland for a recent study of the data, especially p. 101.

[67]There are also two localities called *Emondeville* and a former *Amondetot*, cf. J. A. des Gautries, pp. 375–6.

[68]J. A. des Gautries, pp. 387–9.

[69]J. A. des Gautries, p. 156; Björkman, pp. 296–7.

[70]J. A. des Gautries, pp. 140–1, 416.

[71]In England ON [y] appears to have been treated as native Eng. [y], as in ME *bür, bir* 'strong wind', *fylcian* 'to collect', *flütten, flitten* 'to carry', cf. OIcel. *byr-r, fylkja, flytja*. See Björk-

man, p. 294. In Ireland, the ONorw. vowel was treated as Irish [ui] and also as [i], as in *lipting, lifting* (OIcel. *lypting* 'raised deck'). See Marstrander, p. 72. In England [ȳ] from earlier |iũ] appears with *i*, as in ME *lire* 'face', *mire* 'ant', *skīe* 'sky' (cf. OIcel. *hlȳr, mýra, ský*). See Björkman, p. 296. In words where Old Icelandic had [ȳ], resulting from *i*-mutation of [ū], Irish words had [iũ]. A certain parallelism between the Irish and the French treatment of this vowel would seem to indicate that the mutation had not yet taken place completely in Scandinavia at the time Ireland and Neustria were settled by the Vikings. Cf. Irish *stiuir* (from ON, cf. OIcel. *stýri* 'rudder'), *stiurusmand* (from ON, cf. OIcel. *stýri-maðr* 'steersman') and the name *Diure* related to OIcel. *Dýri*. In Ireland, the Norse words must have been at the older stage [iũ]. See Marstrander, p. 73, and cf. §25 s.v. ONorm. *estiere* 'rudder'.

[72]T. D. Kendrick, *A History of the Vikings*, p. 219.

[73]Cf. the lexicon, §120.

[74]Cf. Alan Ross, "Old Norse Diphthongs in English", *Acta Philologica Scandinavica*, XIV (1940), 1–10.

[75]But cf. J. A. des Gautries, p. 16, who states that it was in the course of the 10th century after the arrival of the large mass of Scandinavian immigrants in Normandy that this difference between Danish and Norwegian began; i.e. [ei] was retained in Norwegian, but was reduced to [ē] in Danish.

[76]Cf. Pope, p. 163 and Anders Pedersen. *loc. cit.*, p. 90.

[77]Cf. A. Longnon, p. 289.

[78]Cf. Anders Pedersen, *loc. cit.*, p. 96.

[79]Cf. J. A. des Gautries, pp. 126, 145.

[80]Cf. Skautrup, I, 124.

[81]Longnon, pp. 298–9 and Dauzat, *Revue de philologie française et de littérature*, XXXVIII (1926), 112 also see West Germanic influence in these forms. Skautrup, I, 104 stresses the importance of the ODan. nasal vowel in the development of the Norman names in question. In England the name *Ásketill* appeared as *Asketel, Osketel, Askil*, etc. without the nasal vowel. The ON name *Áleif-r* appeared in Ireland as *Amlaiph, Amlaib*, etc. This may mean that the Irish and the Romance speakers had the nasal vowel, whereas the English did not. J. A. des

Gautries, pp. 181–189 states that ONorm. *Ansfred, Ansger* and *Ansgot* may be Norse or West Germanic.

[82]For example, the nasal vowel in ON *há-r* 'dogfish' does not seem to have had any effect on the Norman forms of this word, but it would have been phonetically impossible in OF to have [ã] before [r] in a monosyllabic word.

INDEX

FRENCH AND NORMAN WORDS

F

fale 115
falle 115
falle-rouge 115
fallu 115
falue 115
farcoste 31
fart 300
farter 300
farteur 300
Fermanville 126
feste 32
fete 32
fétonnage 32
fétonner 32
fétonnerie 32
fétonnier 32
feurole 281
fiord 298
fjord 298
flâne 257
flânée 257
flâner 257
flânerie 257
flâneur 257
flânier 257
flanner 257
flatir 258
flèche 116
fliche 116
flie 84
flio 117
flion 84
flique 116
fllagné 257
fllandre 85
fllanneter 257
fllonde 85
fllot 62
floc 117

flonde 85
flondre 85
floner 259
flonise 259
flonné 259
floquet 117
flot 62
floton 33
flottabilité 33
flottable 33
flottage 33
flotte 33
Flottemanville 127
flottement 33
flotter 33
flotteur 33
flouette 219
fuirole 281
furole 281
furolle 281
furoller 281
furolles 281
fuyrolle 281

G

gab 260
gabance 260
gabe 260
gabel 260
gabele 260
gabeler 260
gabelet 260
gabement 260
gaberie 260
gaberise 260
gabesse 260
gabet 260
gabeux 260
gabil 260

INDEX

SCANDINAVIAN WORDS

Alphabetical Order of Words in the Scandinavian Languages.

a á b c ð d e é f g h i í j k l m n o ó

p r s t u ú v x y ý z þ æ œ ǫ ø ä å

(All words are given in their OIcel. spelling, unless otherwise specified. The orthography is that of Ferdinand Holthausen, *Vergleichendes und etymologisches Wörterbuch des Altwestnordischen* (Göttingen, 1948), with the exception of ′ which we are using instead of ‾ for long vowels).

BIBLIOGRAPHIES

1. *Dictionaries, Linguistic Atlases, Encyclopedias, and Place-name Collections.*

BATTISTI, Carlo, and ALESSIO, Giovanni, *Dizionario etimologico italiano* (Florence, 1950-).

BARBE, L., *Dictionnaire du patois normand en usage à Louviers et dans les environs* (Louviers, 1907).

BEAUCOUDREY, R.-G. de, *Le Langage normand au début du xxᵉ siècle, noté sur place dans le canton de Percy (Manche)*, (Paris, n.d. 1911).

BLOCH, Oscar, and WARTBURG, Walther von, *Dictionnaire étymologique de la langue française* (Paris, 1950).

BLÖNDAL, Sigfús, *Islandsk-Dansk Ordbok* (Rejkjavik, 1920–1924).

CLEASBY, Richard, and VIGFUSSON, Gudbrand, *An Icelandic-English Dictionary* (Oxford, 1874).

COTGRAVE, Randle, *A Dictionarie of the French and English Tongues*, reproduced from the first edition (London, 1611), University of South Carolina Press (1950).

DAUZAT, Albert, *Dictionnaire étymologique de la langue française*, 3rd ed. (Paris, 1946).

DECORDE, J., *Dictionnaire du patois du pays de Bray*, (Paris, 1852).

DELBOULLE, A., *Glossaire de la Vallée d'Yères pour servir à l'intelligence du dialecte haut-normand et à l'histoire de la vieille langue française* (Le Havre, 1876).

DIDEROT, Denis, *Encyclopédie* (Lausanne, 1780), XXIII, 118–119.

DIEZ, Friedrich, *Etymologisches Wörterbuch der romanischen Sprachen* (Bonn, 1853).

DU CANGE, C. Fresne, *Glossarium mediae et infimae latinitatis* (Paris, 1883–1887).

DUMÉRIL, Edélestand and Alfred, *Dictionnaire du patois normand* (Caen, 1849).

EGILSSON, Sveinbjörn, and JÓNSSON, Finnur, *Lexicon Poeticum antiquae linguae septentrionalis* (Copenhagen, 1913–1916).

EKWALL, Eilert, *The Oxford Book of English Place-Names* (Oxford, 1936).

FALK, Hjalmar, and TORP, Alf, *Norwegisch-Dänisches Etymologisches Wörterbuch*, (Heidelberg, 1910).

FERRAND, David, *La Muse Normande*, V (glossary), ed. A. Héron, (Rouen, 1895).

Franck's Etymologisch Woordenboek der Nederlandsche Taal, ed. Dr. N. Van Wijk (The Hague, 1929).

FRESNAY, A. G. de, *Mémento ou recueil courant de divers mots, expressions et locutions tirés du patois normand en usage dans le pays de Caux et particulièrement dans le canton de Tôtes* (Rouen, 1881).

FRITZNER, J., *Ordbog over det gamle norske Sprog*, 2nd ed. (Christiania, 1886–1896).

GAMILLSCHEG, Emil, *Etymologisches Wörterbuch der französischen Sprache* (Heidelberg, 1928).

GAUTRIES, Jean Adigard des, *Les Noms de personnes scandinaves en Normandie de 911 à 1066*, Nomina Germanica 11 (Lund, 1954).

GILLIÉRON, Jules, and EDMONT, Edmond, *Atlas linguistique de la France* and *Supplément I* (Paris, 1902–1920).

Glossaire du patois jersiais, Société Jersiaise (Saint-Hélier, 1924).

GODEFROY, Frédéric, *Dictionnaire de l'ancien français* (Paris, 1881–1902).

....................., *Lexique de l'ancien français*, reprinted (New York, 1928).

GUERLIN DE GUER, Charles, *Le Parler populaire dans la commune de Thaon (Calvados)*, École pratique des hautes études, Fasc. 136 (Paris, 1901).

HATZFELD, Adolphe, DARMSTETER, Arsène, and THOMAS, Antoine, *Dictionnaire général de la langue française* (Paris, 1892–1900).

HELLQUIST, Elof, *Svensk Etymologisk Ordbok*, 3rd. ed. (Lund, 1948).

HOLTHAUSEN, Ferdinand, *Etymologisches Wörterbuch der englischen Sprache* (Göttingen, 1948).

HOLTHAUSEN, Ferdinand, *Vergleichendes und etymologisches Wörterbuch des Altwestnordischen* (Göttingen, 1948).

HUGUET, Edmond, *Dictionnaire de la langue française du seizième siècle* (Paris, 1925-).

JAKOBSEN, Jakob, *An Etymological Dictionary of the Norn Language in Shetland* (London-Copenhagen, 1928-1932).

JAL, Auguste, *Glossaire nautique* (Paris, 1848).

JORET, Charles, *Essai sur le patois du Bessin*, Mémoires de la Société de linguistique III and IV (Paris, 1881–1884).

KALKAR, Otto, *Ordbog til det ældre danske Sprog 1300–1700* (Copenhagen, 1881–1912).

KLUGE, Friedrich, *Etymologisches Wörterbuch der deutschen Sprache* (Berlin, 1951).

........................., *Seemannssprache* (Halle, 1911).

Larousse Mensuel Illustré (Paris, 1907-   ).

LE HÉRICHER, Edouard, *Histoire et glossaire du normand, de l'anglais et de la langue française* (Paris-Avranches, n.d.)

........................., *Normandie scandinave* (Avranches, 1861).

LITTRÉ, Emile, *Dictionnaire de la langue française* (Paris, 1873), *Supplément,* 1877.

LONGNON, Auguste, *Les Noms de lieu de la France* (Paris, 1920–1929).

MANSION, J. E., ed. *Heath's Standard French and English Dictionary* (London, n.d.)

MAZE, Abbé Camille, *Étude sur le langage de la banlieue du Havre* (Paris-Rouen-Le Havre, 1903).

MÉNAGE, G., *Dictionnaire étymologique ou Origines de la langue françoise* (Paris, 1750).

MÉTIVIER, G., *Dictionnaire franco-normand du patois de Guernesey* (London, 1870).

MEYER–LÜBKE, W., *Romanisches Etymologisches Wörterbuch,* 3rd ed. (Heidelberg, 1935).

MOISY, Henry, *Dictionnaire du patois normand* (Caen, 1887).

........................., *Glossaire comparatif anglo-normand* (Caen, 1889).

A New English Dictionary, ed. James Murray (Oxford, 1888–1928).

Nouveau Larousse Illustré, Volumes I–VII and *Supplément* (Paris, n.d.).

Nouveau Larousse Universel (Paris, 1949).

Ordbok over det danske Sprog, grundlagt af Verner Dahlerup (Copenhagen, 1919–   ).

PAASCH, Captain, *De la quille à la pomme du mât* (Paris, 1908).

RAYMOND, *Dictionnaire général de la langue française* (Paris, 1832).

ROBIN, E., *Dictionnaire du patois normand en usage dans le département de l'Eure*, ed. Le Prevost, Passy and de Blosseville (Evreux, 1879).

TOBLER, Adolph–LOMMATZSCH, Erhard, *Altfranzösisches Wörterbuch* (Berlin, 1925–   ).

VALKHOFF, Marius, *Les Mots français d'origine néerlandaise* (Amersfoort, 1931).

VASMER, Max, *Russisches Etymologisches Wörterbuch* (Heidelberg, 1950–   ).

VINCENT, Auguste, *Toponymie de la France* (Brussels, 1937), pp. 158–161.

WARTBURG, Walther von, *Französisches Etymologisches Wörterbuch* (Bonn, 1928–   ).

......................, *Bibliographie des dictionnaires patois* (Paris, 1934).

ZOËGA, Geir T., *A Concise Dictionary of Old Icelandic* (Oxford, 1926).

2. *The French Language: Historical Grammars, Phonetics, Word Studies, etc.*

ALESSIO, Giovanni, *Grammatica Storica Francese*, I (Bari, 1951).

BARBIER, Paul, *English Influence on the French Vocabulary* (Oxford, 1921).

BARTSCH, Karl, *Chrestomathie de l'ancien français* (Leipzig, 1884).

BEAULIEUX, Charles, *Histoire de l'orthographe française* (Paris, 1927).

BERGER, H., *Die Lehnwörter in der französischen Sprache ältester Zeit* (Leipzig, 1899).

BOURCIEZ, Édouard, *Éléments de linguistique romane*, 4th ed. (Paris, 1946).

BRUNOT, Ferdinand, *Histoire de la langue française des origines à 1900*, I (Paris, 1924).

BRUNOT, Ferdinand, and BRUNEAU, Ch., *Précis de grammaire historique de la langue française*, 3rd ed. (Paris, 1949).

BUBEN, Vladimir, *Influence de l'orthographe sur la prononciation du français moderne* (Bratislava, 1935).

BURGHARDT, Ernst, *Über den Einfluss des Englischen auf das Anglonormannische* (Halle, 1906).

COHEN, Marcel, *Histoire d'une langue: le français* (Paris, 1947).

DAUZAT, Albert, *Histoire de la langue française* (Paris, 1930).

........................, *La Toponymie française* (Paris, 1946).

........................, *Les Noms de famille de France* (Paris, 1949).

DIEZ, Friedrich, *Grammatik der romanischen Sprachen*, 1st ed. (Bonn, 1836), 2nd ed. (Bonn, 1856).

EWERT, Alfred, *The French Language* (London, 1933).

FRAHM, W., *Das Meer und die Seefahrt in der altfranzösischen Literatur* (diss. Göttingen, 1914).

GILLIÉRON, Jules, *Généalogie des mots qui désignent l'abeille* (Paris, 1918).

GREDIG, Silvia, *Essai sur la formation du vocabulaire du skieur français* (Zurich, 1939).

HAUDRICOURT, André G., and JUILLAND, Alphonse G., *Essai pour une histoire structurale du phonétisme français* (Paris, 1949).

HOLMES, Urban T., and SCHATZ, Alexander H., *A History of the French Language* (New York, 1938).

HOPFGARTEN, G., *Der Untergang altfranzösischer Wörter germanischer Herkunft* (Halle, 1926).

JORET, Charles, *Des caractères et de l'extension du patois normand* (Paris, 1883).

........................, *Les Noms de lieu non romane et la colonisation scandinave et germanique en Normandie* (Paris, 1913).

........................, *Mélanges de phonétique normande* (Paris, 1884).

KEMNA, K., *Der Begriff "Schiff" im Französischen* (Marburg, 1901).

MACKEL, E., *Die germanischen Elemente in der französischen und provenzalischen Sprache* (Heilbronn, 1887).

Mélanges linguistiques offerts à Gaston Paris (Paris, 1909).

NYROP, Kr., *Grammaire historique de la langue française*, I (Copenhagen, 1904).

POPE, Mildred K., *From Latin to Modern French with especial consideration of Anglo-Norman* (Manchester, 1952).

POPPE, E., *Der Wortschatz des Journal des Sieur de Gouberville in seinen Beziehungen zu den heutigen normannischen Mundarten* (Leipzig, 1936).

RICHTER, Elise, *Chronologische Phonetik des Französischen bis zum Ende des 8. Jahrhunderts, Beihefte zur Zeitschrift für romanische Philologie* (Halle, 1934).

SAGGAU, H., *Die Benennungen der Schiffsteile und Schiffs-geräte im Neufranzösischen* (Kiel, 1905).

SAINÉAN, Lazare, *La Langue de Rabelais* (Paris, 1922–1923).

...................., *Les Sources indigènes de l'étymologie française,* Volumes I-III (Paris, 1925–1930).

SHIPMAN, George Raymond, *The Vowel Phonemes of Meigret,* Monograph Series on Languages and Linguistics, Institute of Languages and Linguistics, School of Foreign Service, Georgetown University (Washington, 1953).

THOMAS, Antoine, *Essais de philologie française* (Paris, 1897).

...................., *Mélanges d'étymologie française* (Paris, 1902).

...................., *Nouveaux Essais de philologie française* (Paris, 1904).

WARTBURG, Walther von, *Die Ausgliederung der romanischen Sprachräume* (Bern, 1950).

...................., *Évolution et structure de la langue française* (Leipzig-Berlin, 1936), 3rd ed. (Bern, 1946).

3. *Scandinavian and other Languages.*

BJÖRKMAN, Erik, *Scandinavian Loan Words in Middle English* (Halle, 1900–1902).

BRØNDAL, Viggo, *Substrater og Laan i Romansk og Germansk* (Copenhagen, 1917).

BRØNDUM-NIELSEN, Johan, *Gammeldansk Grammatik,* I (Co-penhagen, 1928).

DAHLERUP, Verner, *Det Danske Sprogs Historie* (Copenhagen, 1896).

...................., *Geschichte der dänischen Sprache* (Ulm, 1905).

EKWALL, Eilert, "The Scandinavian Element", in *Introduction to the Survey of English Place Names,* ed. A. Mawer and F. M. Stenton (Cambridge, England, 1929), pp. 55–92.

JACOBSEN, Lis, and MOLTKE, Erik, *Danmarks Runeind-skrifter* (Copenhagen, 1942).

LINDKVIST, Harold, *Middle English Place Names of Scan-dinavian Origin* (Uppsala, 1912).

LUICK, Karl, *Historische Grammatik der englischen Sprache* (Leipzig, 1921–1940).

MARSTRANDER, Carl J. S., *Bidrag til det norske Sprogs His-torie i Irland* (Christiania, 1915).

SANDAHL, Bertil, *Middle English Sea Terms*: I, "The Ship's Hull", *Essays and Studies on English Language and Literature*, VIII (Uppsala, 1951).

SEIP, Didrik, *Norsk Språkhistorie til omkring 1370* (Oslo, 1933).

SERJEANTSON, Mary S., *A History of Foreign Words in English* (New York, 1936).

SKAUTRUP, Peter, *Det Danske Sprogs Historie*, I (Copenhagen, 1944).

THOMSEN, Vilhelm, *The Relations between Ancient Russia and Scandinavia* (Oxford, 1874).

4. Historical and Literary Works.

BEAUREPAIRE, Charles de, *La Vicomté de l'eau de Rouen au xiiie et au xive siècle* (Evreux, 1856).

BENOÎT, *La Chronique des Ducs de Normandie*, ed. F. Michel (Paris, 1836–1844).

BERNEVILLE, Guillaume de, *La Vie de Saint Gilles*, ed. G. Paris and Alphonse Bos (Paris, 1881).

BEROUL, *Le Roman de Tristan*, ed. Muret, Société des anciens textes français (Paris, 1903).

La Chançun de Guillelme, ed. H. Suchier (Halle, 1911).

La Chanson de Roland, ed. F. Whitehead (Oxford, 1942); ed. J. Bédier (Paris, 1927).

Dudonis Sancti Quintini de moribus et actis primorum Normanniae ducum, ed. Jules Lair (Paris, 1875).

Edda Snorra Sturlusonar, ed. þorleifr Jónsson (Copenhagen, 1875).

GUILLAUME DE JUMIÈGES, *Gesta Normannorum ducum*, ed. Marx (Paris, 1914).

Guillaume Longue-Épée, ed. J. Lair (Paris, 1893).

Heimskringla, ed. F. Jónsson (Copenhagen, 1911).

KENDRICK, T. J., *Archaeology of the Channel Islands* (Jersey, 1928).

.........................., *A History of the Vikings* (London, 1930).

LECONTE DE LISLE, *Poèmes barbares*, ed. A. Lemerre (Paris, n.d.).

LE PREVOST, A., *Mémoires et notes pour servir à l'histoire du département de l'Eure*, I-III (Evreux, 1862–1869).

LOT, Ferdinand, *Études critiques sur l'abbaye de Saint-Wandrille*, Bibliothèque de l'École des Hautes Études, Sciences historiques et philologiques, Fasciscule 204 (Paris, 1913).

MARIE DE FRANCE, *Lais*, ed. Warnke, Bibliotheca Norman-
nica III, (Halle, 1925).

MARIE DE FRANCE, *Fables*, ed. Warnke, Bibliotheca Nor-
mannica VI, 3rd ed. (Halle, 1898).

POOLE, Austin Lane, *From Domesday Book to Magna Carta*
(Oxford, 1951).

PRENTOUT, Henri, *L'Histoire de Normandie* (Caen, 1929).

RONCIÈRE, Charles de la, *Histoire de la marine française*, I
(Paris, 1899), pp. 93–137.

TARDIF, Ernest-Joseph, *Coutumiers de Normandie*, II (Rouen-
Paris, 1896).

La Vie de Saint Alexis, ed. Gaston Paris (Paris, 1911).

VOGEL, Walther, *Die Normannen und das Fränkische Reich
bis zur Gründung der Normandie (799–911)* (Heidelberg,
1906).

WACE, Robert, *Le Roman de Brut*, ed. Ivor Arnold (Paris,
1938–1940).

WACE, Robert, *Le Roman de Rou*, ed. Hugo Andresen (Heilbronn, 1879).

5. *Articles.*

ASKEBERG, Fritz, "La Guerche, ett Bidrag till Loireviking-
arnas Historia", *Namn och Bygd*, XXXII (Upsala, 1944),
176–203.

BAIST, G., "Germanische Seemannswörter in der französischen
Sprache", *Zeitschrift für deutsche Wortforschung*, IV
(Strassburg, 1903), 257–277.

BARBIER, Paul, "Miscellanea lexicographica, Etymological and
Lexicographical Notes on the French Language and on the
Romance Dialects of France", *Proceedings of the Leeds
Philosophical and Literary Society* (Leeds, 1927–1947).

........................., "Noms de poissons. Notes étymologiques et lexico-
graphiques", *Revue des langues romanes*, LI, LII, LIII,
LIV, LVII, LVIII, LXIII, LXV (Montpellier-Paris, 1908–
1927).

........................., "Notes on Germanic Initial *w* in French and in
the French dialects", *Zeitschrift für französische Sprache und
Literatur*, LIII (Oppeln, 1929–1930), 1–25.

BOUARD, Michel de, "La Hague, camp retranché des Vikings?",
Annales de Normandie, III (Caen, 1953), 3–14.

BRØNDAL, Viggo, "Les Normands et la langue des vikings", *Normannia*, X (Caen, 1930), 147–153.

BRUCH, J., "Die bisherige Forschung über die germanischen Einflüsse auf die romanischen Sprachen", *Revue de linguistique romane*, II (Paris, 1926), 25–98.

COLLIN, Zacharias, "Examen critique des étymologies islandaises proposées dans le Dictionnaire du patois normand de MM Duméril", *Lund Universitets Årsskrift*, III (Lund, 1864), 1–22.

DAUZAT, A., "Essais de géographie linguistique", *Revue de philologie française et de littérature*, XXXVIII (Paris, 1926).

.........................., "Le Substrat germanique dans l'évolution phonétique du français", *Mélanges de linguistique et de philologie offerts à J. van Ginneken* (Paris, 1937).

DELBOULLE, A., "Notes lexicologiques", *Romania*, XXXIII (Paris, 1904), 346.

EMANUELLI, F., "Le parler populaire de l'île anglo-normande d'Aurigny", *Revue de philologie française et de littérature*, XX-XXI (Paris, 1907–1908).

FALK, H., "Altnordisches Seewesen", *Wörter und Sachen*, IV (Heidelberg, 1912), 1–122.

FLOM, George T., "On the History of Views about the Vowel System of Old Norse", *Journal of English and Germanic Philology*, XXXVIII (Urbana, 1939).

FOUCHÉ, P., "Les noms de lieux normands en -beuf, -fleur et le nom de *l'île d'Yeu*", *Revue internationale d'onomastique*, IV (Paris, 1952), 161–167.

GAUTRIES, Jean Adigard des, "Les noms en -torp", *Études germaniques*, VI (Paris, 1951), 3–10; "Les Caudecotte", *Études germaniques*, III (Paris, 1953), 1–5.

.........................., "Les Noms de lieux de la Manche attestés entre 911 et 1066", *Annales de Normandie*, I (Caen, 1951), 9–44.

.........................., "Les Noms de lieux du Calvados attestés entre 911 et 1066", *Annales de Normandie*, II, 209–228; III, 22–36, 135–148 (Caen, 1952–1953).

.........................., "Les Noms de lieux des îles anglo-normandes attestés entre 911 et 1066", *Annales de Normandie*, II (Caen, 1952), 27–33.

GUERLIN DE GUER, Charles, "Introduction à l'atlas linguistique de la Normandie, du Maine, et du Perche", *Le Français moderne*, XIII (Paris, 1945), 19–68, and 249–269.

HOLMBERG, Bengt, "Tomt och Toft som appellativ och ort-namnselement", *Skrifter utgivna av Kungl. Gustav Adolfs Akademien*, XVII (Uppsala, 1946).

HOLMBOE, J., "Et gammelt norsk plantenavn i Normandiet", *Maal og Minne* (Oslo, 1929), 108–114.

JAKOBSEN, Jakob, "Stednavne og Personnavne i Normandiet med særlight Hensyn til den Nordiske Bosættelse", *Danske Studier* (Copenhagen, 1911), 59–84.

LACROIX, Jean-Yves, "Le Ski tel qu'on le parle", *Vie et langage*, XII (Paris, 1953), 138–141.

LECHANTEUR, Fernand, "Un Curieux vestige des déplacements normands", *Annales de Normandie*, III (Caen, 1953), 194.

...................., "Bosc et bois dans les noms de lieux de la Nor-mandie", *Annales de Normandie*, II (Caen, 1952), 65–72.

...................., "Les Mots et les choses", *Annales de Normandie*, I (Caen, 1951), 99–109.

...................., "Matronymes en Basse Normandie", *Actes et mémoires du 3e congrès de toponymie et d'anthroponymie*, III (Louvain, 1951), 778–786.

LE VAVASSEUR, G., "Remarques sur quelques expressions usitées en Normandie, leur emploi par certains auteurs, leur origine, leur étymologie, etc.", *Annuaire des cinq départements de la Normandie* (Caen, 1878), 121–224.

MARQUAND, E. D., "The Guernsey Dialect and its Plant Names", *Transactions of the Guernsey Society of Natural Science and Local Research*, V (St. Pierre Port, 1905), 37–47; "The Guernsey Dialect Names of Birds, Fishes, In-sects, etc.", VI (1906), 512–531.

MARTINET, André, "Celtic Lenition and Western Romance Consonants", *Language*, XXVIII (Baltimore, 1952), 192–217.

...................., "Occlusives and Fricatives with Reference to some Problems of Romance Philology", *Word*, V (New York, 1949), 116–122.

...................., reviews of works by W. von Wartburg, *Word*, VII (1951), 73–76, and R. Menéndez-Pidal, *Word*, VIII (1952), 182–186.

MUSSET, Lucien, "Les Surnoms normands en -*man*", *Études germaniques*, II (1947), 133–143.

NYROP, K., "Ein vermeintliches Wikingerwort", *Wörter und Sachen*, VII (Heidelberg, 1921), 81–101.

......................, "Et formentligt Vikingerord," *Aarbøger for nordisk Oldkyndighed og Historie*, 3rd series, IX (Copenhagen, 1919), 1–34.

PEDERSEN, Anders, "Nogle Normanniske Lydforhold", *Danske Studier* (Copenhagen, 1911), pp. 85–98.

PETERSEN, Niels Matthias, "Bemaerkninger om Stedsnavne i Normandiet", *Nordisk Tidsskrift for Oldkyndighed*, II (Copenhagen, 1833), reprinted in N. M. Petersen, *Samlede Afhandlinger*, I (Copenhagen, 1870).

ROSS, Alan, "Old Norse Diphthongs in English", *Acta Philologica Scandinavica*, XIV (Copenhagen, 1940), 1–10.

SINEL, Joseph, "The Fishes of the Channel Islands", *Transactions of the Guernsey Society of Natural Science and Local Research*, V (St. Pierre Port, 1905), 57–60.

SJÖGREN, A., "Le Genre des mots d'emprunt norrois en normand", *Romania*, LIV (Paris, 1928), 381–412.

SOUILLET, Guy, "La Guerche. Le problème de la marche franco-bretonne", *Mémoires de la société d'histoire et d'archéologie de Bretagne*, XXIV (Rennes, 1944), 25–46.

STENTON, F. M., "The Scandinavian Colonies in England and Normandy", *Transactions of the Royal Historical Society*, 4th series, XXVII (London, 1945), 1–12.

TILANDER, Gunnar, "Guillaume", *Studia neophilologica*, XXIII (Uppsala, 1950–1951), 145–149.

VERRIER, P., "Origine et évolution des anciennes diphtongues françaises", *Romania*, LXII (Paris, 1936), 289–301.

VOGEL, Walther, "Nordische Seefahrten im früheren Mittelalter", *Meereskunde*, I (Berlin, 1907), 1–40.

WAHLGREN, Ernst G., "Anc. Franç. *isnel, ignel*", *Studia neophilologica*, III (Uppsala, 1930–1931), 116–129.

WALBERG, E., "Sur un mot français d'origine nordique", *Studia neophilologica*, XVI (Uppsala, 1943), 39–49.

WARTBURG, Walther von, "Der Einfluss der germanischen Sprachen auf den französischen Wortschatz", *Archiv für Kulturgeschichte*, XX (Berlin, 1930), 309–325.

WOLEDGE, B., "Notes on Wace's Vocabulary", *Modern Language Review*, XLVI (Cambridge, 1951), 16–30.

Bauermeister
17.iv.59